Across All Worlds
Jesus Inside Our Darkness

Across All Worlds
Jesus Inside Our Darkness

An essay on reconciliation
in honor of Professor James B. Torrance

C. Baxter Kruger, Ph. D.

PERICHORESIS PRESS
Jackson, MS

For J. B.,
in gratitude.

Across All Worlds

Across all worlds
He came for us
With Father's passion burning

With strength unknown
In Spirit's fire
He fought for our undoing

What love, what care
What fearless joy
Has found us in the night

That we may know
As he has known
The everlasting light

Awake, My child
Your fear lay down
There's hope for which you long

The night is day
The Son has come
The Father's heart is strong

−C. Baxter Kruger, 2003

Perichoresis, Inc.
P.O. Box 98157
Jackson, MS 39298 U.S.A

For more information about Perichoresis visit
www.perichoresis.org

ISBN-10: 0-9645465-6-6
ISBN-13: 978-0-9645465-6-1

Table of Contents

A Note from Professor Alan Torrance

On the afternoon of Saturday, November 15, 2003, my eldest son, Andrew, decided on the spur of the moment to visit his grandparents in Edinburgh. My father (in memory of whom this book was written) was thrilled to see him, embraced him at the door and welcomed him into his home—which he invariably made everyone else's home. On this occasion, he decided to sit Andrew down and share with him the theological affirmations which so invigorated and enthused him and out of which he had lived his life. There was nothing more liberative and transformative for Dad than the good news of the grace of God—that we are accepted and embraced unconditionally in Christ, that we are forgiven before we even ask and that God's purposes for us are that we might discover this and be freed by it to love and forgive one another unconditionally. The conversation continued for over an hour but was brought to a close when my father suddenly and unexpectedly felt unwell. Prior to heading upstairs to lie down, he gave Andrew a present of Baxter Kruger's book, *Jesus and the Undoing of Adam* and urged him to read it. As he climbed the stairs, Dad enthused to my mother about the wonderful conversation he had just had with Andrew. An hour or so later, he was to know the embrace of his heavenly Father in all its fullness. When I arrived later that evening, I found Andrew sitting speechless with loss. In his hand was the final present he had received from his grandfather.

It would be impossible to exaggerate my father's enthusiasm for Baxter Kruger's work and writing. It gave him untold excitement and he talked about the Perichoresis Press continually. One of the texts that my father continually cited to me was the famous exhortation that we find in Deuteronomy 11—that we must pass on to the next generation the good news of God's covenantal commitment to his people, the deliverance from slavery that is ours and the implications of this for how we should live as liberated people: "You shall therefore lay up these words of mine in your heart . . . . And you shall teach them to your children, talking of them when you are sitting in your house, and when you are walking by the way, and when you lie down and when you rise. And you shall write them upon the doorposts of your house and upon your gates."

My father was living this out on that final afternoon. And what gave him such pleasure about Baxter Kruger's books was the imaginative but also profound way in which he was passing on this liberating and transforming Gospel to our generation.

Across All Worlds is a superb book which I personally shall be recommending, as I have his other Perichoresis publications, wherever I go.

Professor Alan J. Torrance
Chair of Systematic Theology
St Mary's College, University of St Andrews
Scotland

Foreword

In working as a Family Physician, one encounters people of all strata, colours, and creeds, and on some occasions we are privileged to meet their inner worlds. In these self-revealing times, one is struck by the universality of the human innards. The chief landmarks encountered are fear, rejection, guilt, trauma, and their various shameful combinations, covered in layers of defence mechanisms. These blended emotions are woven as threads through our states of being and are involved in both the actions and reactions of our lives.

Does the gospel have anything to say to the average suffering person, plodding through life in such pain? Is Jesus Christ merely a concept, a doctrine that helps people hope to avoid hell?

What is our healing? What is salvation? Or perhaps, who is our salvation and how does he heal?

It is into the existential reality of human pain that Jesus and his gospel of the Triune God speak and heal.

One of the early Church's great fathers, St. Gregory of Nazianzus, argued that "the unassumed is the unhealed." He was making clear that if any of the darkness or pain of our fallen human existence was not entered by Christ, then it would not participate in the great healing exchange, where Christ gave us his life and his relationship with his Father and took our darkness into himself. Our healing took place in Jesus' own experience. He is our healing and he is our salvation. Healing and salvation are one.

Amongst others, T. F. Torrance and later C. Baxter Kruger have written on this in their respective books *The Mediation of Christ* and *Jesus and the Undoing of Adam*.

This understanding of Christ taking on and healing our fallen humanity is a source of joy for many, but does it have anything to offer us in our brokenness, beyond being a cognitive concept? Is it only doctrine? Is it more than a doctrine? In line with ancient thought, Dr.

Kruger begins in the affirmative and unpacks this healing in *Across All Worlds*.

Inside our beings, behind the layers of our defence mechanisms, pain arises from deep parts of us like smoke from the fires of our subterranean and hidden brokenness. In these areas we believe that we "are not" acceptable in one form or another. In this state we are unable to help ourselves. We are trapped in our own vision of god and cannot see the acceptance of the Father.

It is in this deep, helpless state that we are met by Jesus Christ. He is the one who knows the Father. And he is not distant. Jesus is at the core of all our being and he is beyond all. As he is in the deepest parts of us, he is able to share what he knows of his Father with us behind our defences and beyond our volitional attempts to heal ourselves. Jesus' freedom to meet us in our darkness with his own knowledge of his Father is the heart of this book.

Jesus Christ is not a doctrine, but a person who knows his Father. If this trinitarian-incarnational understanding/revelation becomes only a doctrine, that would be a tragedy of the most serious proportions. We would be left with ourselves and another empty theological trend.

One does not just write love songs and poetry, or papers on the topic of love. People engage in the soul-baring process of being loved and loving each other. This is an ontological truth and experience. Love is about persons in relation, and so it is with Jesus Christ and us.

Jesus is a person, and he shares with us his knowledge of the Father that no one else has or has had. He shares his heart and mind and being with us. To reduce and truncate this personal sharing to a doctrine robs people of the power of the gospel, as it robs them of the Father's love in Jesus and his relational healing. Without knowing the unconditional acceptance of the Father in Jesus, we are not able to drop our defence mechanisms, and as a consequence we will not allow our souls to receive His love and heal.

Laying out this truth of "Christ in us" is a broad highway to help avoid the unengaged, life-useless, doctrinal cul-de-sac.

Across All Worlds takes this ancient truth and reality of "Christ in us" and breaches Western cognitive dualism to help us engage our hearts and bodies in Jesus' relationship with us.

May Jesus Christ meet your deepest inner needs as you read.

Bruce Wauchope, M.D.
Bedford Medical Clinic
Adelaide, Australia

Preface

Jesus wants his Father known. He is passionate about it. He cannot bear for us to live without knowing his Father, without knowing his heart, his lavish embrace, his endless love—and the sheer freedom *to be* that works within us as we see his Father's face. Jesus knows the Father from all eternity. He sits at His right hand and sees Him face to face, and shares life and all things with Him in the fellowship of the Spirit. How could he be content to leave us in the dark with no vision of his Father's heart? How could this Son be indifferent when we are so lost and afraid and bound in our mythology? Burning with the Father's love for us, inspired with the Spirit's fire, the Son ran to embrace our broken existence, baptizing himself into our blindness. He braved the seas of our darkness to come to us. Why? So that he could share with us his own communion with his Father in the Spirit, and we could know the Father with him, and taste and feel and experience life in His embrace.

This book is about Jesus Christ finding us, and finding us in our fallen minds. He is not up there somewhere, watching us from a distance. He is not waiting for the day when he can become a factor in our lives. We tend to think that people are separated from Jesus, and that at some point folks pray to receive an absent Jesus into their lives. The truth is other way around. Jesus has received us into his life. We don't make him part of our world; he has made us a part of his. He has included us in the abounding life he shares with his Father and in his anointing with the Spirit. And the *us* he has included is not the perfect us, not the untarnished version that we present to the world and hope everyone believes. The *us* he has included is the broken us, the wounded, tired, and scared us, the self-centered, self-protecting, hiding us. So we are in for a wild ride. For Jesus is determined that the broken us comes to know his Father's love in the freedom of the Spirit. He won't give up.

We want a quick fix, but that is not how it works. For the life Jesus lives with his Father and Spirit and the life we live in our darkness don't fit together like a hand in a glove. Jesus has forever included us in his world, but we are scared to death, and we bring with us a deeply alienated way of looking at things, a profound wrong-headedness and confusion. If we are to come to experience Jesus' Father and His endless love, we must face why we don't. We must face our wrong-headedness, our pretending, running and hiding, and our warped view of God, others and life itself. *And that hurts.*

In the end, and at all points in between, we face a simple choice. We either embrace the good hurt, the life-giving and liberating pain of our enlightenment in Jesus, which gives way to sheer joy in the Father's embrace, or we continue to live in our own worlds, where our way of seeing things produces deeper and deeper alienation and brokenness and misery. In the meantime, we live in the crucible between the pain of our self-destructive vision and the liberating hurt of the Father's love, the love that Jesus shares with us. Jesus has pledged to walk it out with us until we know as he knows, until all we see is his Father's face. That is reconciliation.

I have always known that the God question and human wholeness go together. The search to find out how took me across the Atlantic to the feet of Professor James B. Torrance. It was Professor Torrance (or J. B. as we called him) who taught me that the *relationship* of the Father, Son, and Spirit is the heart of the New Testament and of creation itself. He gave me a new prescription for my glasses and told me to use it. He challenged me to rethink my theology from the ground up in the light of this truth of all truths. Like our Father in heaven, he never once abandoned his students as we struck out to think and pray and live.

With this foundational vision, J. B. pointed me to the early Church, especially to John and Paul, the work of Irenaeus and Athanasius, and to the work of modern writers such as George MacDonald, Thomas Erskine, John McLeod Campbell, Karl Barth, Lesslie Newbigin, C. S. Lewis, and not least, the profound work of his own brother, T. F. Torrance. I found here brothers of the same breathtaking vision, brothers whose insights rocked my illusions and demanded serious and deep repentance, brothers who stood me before the stunning beauty of the trinitarian life of Father, Son, and Spirit, and told me that this life was for us all.

I was blessed with an outstanding teacher who knew as much as he loved, who guided me to the great fathers and stood with me in the fire. And I have been blessed with friends who love life and are determined to understand what the gospel of the Father, Son and Spirit means for us here and now—from romance to fishing, from being a parent to having coffee with friends, and not least to our pain. Men like Steve Horn who loves "union with Christ" as much as I do, and who has held my feet to the practical fire, faithfully reminding me that theology is of no value at all if we cannot live it. Dr. Bruce Wauchope has included me in his remarkable journey into human brokenness, spiritual pain, and how our insides work. Gary Arinder has walked me through hundreds of questions about relationships and relational issues in the light of family systems theory. Christy Jones, David Upshaw and Cary Stockett, Robert Lucas, Rod Dumas and Julian Fagan, Bert Gary, Paul Leverenz and David Kowalick, Ken Blue, Dirk Vanderleest, and my faithful wife, Beth, have been constant partners in the endless struggle to know the truth and its freedom.

This book is the expression of the melding of two worlds in me—the stunning and rich vision of trinitarian theology and the pain of the human heart. Neither the two worlds nor their coming together in me happened in a vacuum. The melding is the fruit of 46 years of living and the blessing of a long conversation, theological and practical, stretching across years and oceans. It is impossible therefore to thank everyone who has had a part in the development of my thought. How do you footnote a 25-year conversation? I do, however, want to thank Steve and Bruce and Gary specifically. I am grateful for your friendship. You have stood your ground and fought to know the truth, and you shared your mind and heart with me. This book is as much yours as it is mine.

But most of all I want to thank Professor James B. Torrance for sharing the vision. It is hard to imagine what my life would be like now if the Lord had not led me to your feet. You now know as you are known, a full participant in the conversation and communion you so deeply loved. No more darkness. But, dear brother, you had an awful lot of light when you were here. Thank you for caring, for fighting, for staying the course, and for turning so many hearts toward "the Son's relationship with the Father in the Spirit." I hope this book is an honor to your heart.

C. Baxter Kruger
Father's Day, 2004

All things have been given to Me by My Father;
and no one knows the Son, except the Father;
nor does anyone know the Father, except the Son,
and anyone to whom the Son wills to reveal Him.

—Matthew 11:27

Cutting to the Chase

She sat smoldering as she listened to the shouts.

"I can't believe he said it!" cried the little man with a crooked nose. "The outright arrogance of the man—and he's barely thirty."

"It doesn't surprise me," said Ehud. "I've heard he was radical, even scandalous—and the things I've heard he says about *God,* calling him *Father.*"

"As if *he* would know God," growled the little man.

"Ehud, it was right here on this spot. I heard him with my own ears: 'No one knows the Father, but the Son.'" Invisible fire shot out of Saul's nostrils.

"*Who* does he think he is, saying something like that in Israel?" Ehud sneered.

"There was no mistaking it," shouted Saul. "He even paused, and stared at us to make the point sting. 'No one, not a soul, no other person but me knows God.' That's what he meant. He all but drew a circle on the ground and said that no one but him has ever been in the circle with God at all. *Blasphemy!* Sheer *blasphemy!*"

"What about Abraham? What about Moses? What about David and the prophets?" cried Ehud.

"Right here, Ehud, I tell you, right here is where he said it. He made *Gentiles* out of us Jews! He threw out the whole tradition!"

"Well, he won't last long around here with that kind of nonsense."

"*Nonsense?* It was outright *blasphemy!*" screamed Saul. "The brothers will get him soon enough."

The young woman could bear it no longer. "I thought what Jesus said was *good news,*" she said softly.

"And who are *you?*" sneered Saul, his crooked nose hoisted in the air like a sail.

"My name is Mary Magdalene." The light in her eyes flashed sheer joy, as she stared a hole into Saul. "You folks have it all figured out, but for those of us who don't, Jesus has the answer."

"Who are you to dare speak to us, *woman,* let alone *lecture* us?" Saul scowled.

"Obviously, being a *woman,* and a *sinner,* I am no one to you, but Jesus accepts me. He is the only one who knows the Father, and he brings the Father's love to me."

"Enough! You should be stoned on the spot," growled Saul, as he snatched up his robe, snorted and stormed away. Ehud ran behind him.

Their bitter diatribes rung in Mary's ears as she watched their heads bob back and forth, arms waving, fists clenched in misguided passion.

"I have given *my life* to God," shouted Saul, "and this man has the audacity to tell me I don't even know God."

"And worse," dripped Ehud, "that *he* does, and that he will share *his knowledge* of *the Father* with us."

Such a thought burned like lava in Saul's soul. "This is outrageous! Jesus has lost his mind."

Mary stood silent as she listened. Joy and grief swirled within her. "Lord, they just don't get it. Help them. They see you on one side, and themselves on the other—and they are so proud of what they think they have done for you. Give them new eyes."

"*I am,*" said a voice in her heart.

This flash of hot conversation between Saul and Ehud and a simple woman filled with hope cuts right to the issue. Jesus blew the Jewish mind. It is just that simple. Although steeped in divine revelation, and educated through its fiery trial, nevertheless the Jewish mind could not cope with the presence of Jesus Christ. For his presence meant—and means—the end of all religion, ancient or modern, and its new beginning. Saul felt it to the core of his soul: Either Jesus is crazy or we are. Such is the crisis that Jesus' presence creates. We can continue to go the way of Saul and Ehud, stubbornly clinging to our anxiety-ridden vision of God and to our self-generated salvation schemes, or we can go the way of Mary Magdalene and let Jesus share his Father with us.

"No one knows the Father but the Son." These stunning words of Jesus exclude and incite as much as any words ever uttered. Why make such a statement? What is the point of such absolute exclusivity? Didn't Jesus know that it would offend the Jews, not to mention the rest of the world and the world's religions?

Mary Magdalene got the point and found its joy. It is not about us finding our own way to a distant God. It's about Jesus including us in his exclusive relationship with his Father and Spirit.

Jesus is not another in the long line of religious leaders dispensing divine advice and direction. What is unique about Jesus is his *knowledge* of the Father. I don't mean mere intellectual or academic or theological knowledge. I mean personal, experiential, relational knowledge. He *knows* the Father. He sees the Father's face. He lives in communion with the Father in the Spirit. The shocker about Jesus is that he has no interest whatever in hoarding his exclusive communion with His Father: *His passion is sharing.*

Mark it well: Jesus crossed all worlds to come to us, and he did not come to give us a religious manual to follow, or to leave us with fresh insights about a distant God. He came to give *himself* to us, and all he has and knows. He crossed all worlds to establish a personal relationship with us, to include us in his own relationship with his Father and Spirit. He came to share his soul with us, and thus his own knowledge of his Father, his own peace, his own assurance and hope and joy, so that we could know what he knows, so that we could taste and feel and experience the life he alone lives with his Father in the fellowship of the Spirit.

Don't you see? Jesus does not set the example of courage or faith or love and then command us to go and do likewise. He does not define joy and then tell us how to apply it to our lives. He does not give us ten steps to bring in the kingdom, or seven ways to have a relationship with God like he has. What Jesus does is far better, and more shocking, personal, and scary. Before he ever commands, he *shares.* He takes his own knowledge of his Father and shares it with us. He takes his own courage and love, his own faith and peace and joy, and shares them with us, and then commands us to live in them. "Peace I leave with you; *my own peace.* I do not give as the world gives. Therefore let not your heart be troubled, nor let it be fearful" (John 14:27). "These things I have spoken to you that *my joy* may be in you, and your joy made be made full" (John 15:11). "And I have made Your name known to them, and will make it known, that *the love* with which You love me may be *in them,* and *I in them*" (John 17:26). "In the world you have tribulation, but take courage; I have overcome the world" (John 16:33).

As the late Professor James Torrance put it so wonderfully: "The Father has given to us the Son and the Spirit to draw us into a life of shared communion—of participating through the Spirit in the Son's communion with the Father—that we might be drawn in love into the very trinitarian life of God."[1]

The truth that Jesus himself has crossed all worlds to include us in his exclusive relationship with his Father, and the fact that he has done so forever, means that there is far more going on in our lives than we ever dared to dream. We are involved in the trinitarian life of God. We belong to the Father, Son, and Spirit. Such belonging, such inclusion, such involvement is the most wonderful news in the universe, but it also translates into a long, haunting, scary, nowhere-to-hide crisis.

You can see the crisis in Saul and Ehud. They had their own vision of God and their own religion to go with it. They wanted Jesus to repent. They wanted him to drop his vision of God and affirm theirs. He wouldn't. So they lived in the crisis of his presence. We do too.

We live in a relationship with Jesus Christ. In this relationship Jesus is sharing his own communion with his Father and Spirit with us. But it makes no sense to our minds. It is foreign to the way we think—*inconceivable*. Like Saul and Ehud, we are bent on assimilating Jesus into our existing vision. But we can't. So the presence of the Son who knows the Father cuts to the chase of our lives, commanding a vast reinterpretation of everything we thought we knew.

The crisis is a conflict of vision. Either Jesus has lost his mind or we have. Life is where that argument plays out.

---

[1] James B. Torrance, *Worship, Community and the Triune God of Grace* (Carlisle: Paternoster Press; Downers Grove, IL: Intervarsity Press, 1996), 25, 36.

Part 1

Blind as Bats

Chapter 1

The Great Disaster

I will come back to the stunning truth that Jesus Christ shares himself and all he is and has with us, and to what such a gift means to us in our lives, but we cannot get there until we think hard on something else. When Jesus says, "No one knows the Father but the Son," he is making a penetrating statement about the problem of sin and reconciliation. Most of us have been trained to think of sin in legal terms as breaking the Ten Commandments. But when Jesus declares "no one knows the Father but the Son," he is confronting us with a far more devastating notion of sin than that of breaking the law. Let me put it this way: If eternal life is knowing the Father, as Jesus teaches us (John 17:3), then eternal death is not knowing the Father, and sin is the cause of our not knowing. Sin has to do with being blind, with being so profoundly wrong-headed that it is impossible for us to know the Father.[2]

---

[2] My discussion of the fallen mind and the inevitable pain involved in reconciliation grows out of my intense study of the works of Professor T. F. Torrance. One of his greatest contributions to Christian thought, in my opinion, is his steadfast refusal to separate revelation and reconciliation—knowing God and conversion. In holding together the unveiling of God and our need for conversion to perceive the truth, Professor Torrance—along with his brother James—have generated a fresh theological vision and a new series of far-reaching questions. It is not accidental that as we try to think through these issues we find kindred souls in the great leaders of the early Church. Of particular importance here are T. F. Torrance's books, *The Mediation of Christ* (Grand Rapids: Eerdmans Publishing Co., reprint, 1982), *Space, Time and Resurrection* (Edinburgh: The Handsel Press, 1976), *The Trinitarian Faith* (Edinburgh: T & T Clark, 1988), and his essay "The Atoning Obedience of Christ" (*Moravian Theological Seminary Bulletin*, 1959, pp. 65–81). For further reading see the writings of St. Irenaeus and St. Athanasius and the suggestions for further reading at the back of this book, and my book, *The Great Dance* (Jackson, Mississippi: Perichoresis Press, 2000 and Vancouver: Regent College Publishing, 2005).

The problem of sin and reconciliation is far larger than the issue of our being lawbreakers. As my friend Paul Leverenz says, "No matter how many laws we have broken, and no matter how much punishment these acts supposedly deserve, the problem is far more catastrophic." Sin goes way beyond disobedience. The deepest problem of sin is that it makes us utterly incapable of knowing the Father. It afflicts us with such a dastardly wrong-headedness that we cannot know the Father's heart. It makes us so blind that it is impossible for us to see the Father's face. And without knowing the Father's heart, we have no basis for real assurance or hope in our lives at all. If we cannot see His face, we have no possibility of living in the freedom of His abounding love, and in the security and joy of His lavish and eternal embrace.

Reconciliation is not about punishment. Reconciliation is about the Father reaching us in His Son in the Spirit. It is about the Son crossing all the worlds of our confusion to establish a real relationship with us inside our darkness, so that our fallen minds can be converted and we can know the Father and live.

The biblical story is driven by the love of the triune God, and in this love by the *relationship* between God, on the one side, and Adam, Israel, and humanity on the other. In this relationship, the Father speaks. He reveals. He gives. Humanity is thereby summoned to hear, to know, and to receive the Father's love. And in hearing the Father's voice, in knowing His affirmation and receiving His love, humanity is quickened with an abounding life that it can neither possess in itself nor create. This abounding life then overflows into our relationships with one another and with the whole creation.

As creatures, we do not have life in ourselves. Life is a gift. We are designed, or *wired,* to experience life in fellowship with the Father and in *soul knowledge* of His delight and pleasure. Note carefully: There is an infinite difference between religious obedience to a divine being or a divine rule and soul knowledge of the Father's heart. When we know the Father's delight, something happens to us, something that we cannot do to ourselves, something far deeper than the ability to do right: We are quickened with hope. In seeing the Father's true face, our souls are baptized with an unearthly assurance, with a security and confidence not of this world. With this assurance comes an awakening, and with the awakening comes freedom—freedom to stand up, to walk, to risk, to venture forth.

But this is only the beginning. With our Father's assurance comes freedom to give and to receive, freedom to know and to be known, freedom to love and to be loved, and in this freedom real relationships are formed, creativity is unleashed, and creation finds for itself a true friend. This is how the blessed kingdom of the triune God works. We are designed to be quickened with life through spiritual knowledge of the Father's heart, and then for this life to overflow in other-centered love for others and all creation.

But what happens to us if we cannot hear the Father's voice? What happens to Adam, to Israel, to the human race at large? What happens to the relationships between us and creation if we cannot see His face? What happens if we become so wrong-headed and blind that we cannot possibly know the Father's heart, and thus cannot receive His endless love and believe He will never forsake us?

The great disaster of Adam and Eve was not simply that they sinned or were disobedient to a divine rule. The disaster was that in believing the lie of the evil one they became blind. And by "blind," I do not mean that they could not see physically. I mean that their perception of reality became skewed—so skewed that they could no longer perceive the real truth about God or about themselves.

Now if we are designed to experience life in knowing the Father's heart, in hearing his voice of affirmation and joy, and in perceiving His lavish embrace, then becoming blind to the Father is the single greatest disaster that could possibly happen to us.

Adam and Eve moved from hearing and knowing and receiving the Father's love to hiding in fear in the bushes. Their inner vision became so terribly alienated—*so fallen*—that they no longer had a clear perception of the Father's heart at all. And worse, in the place of the Father's heart, their fallen minds invented a new god, a mythological deity, who struck terror in their hearts and baptized their souls with anxiety and hopelessness. They hid: hid from this deity, hid from themselves, and hid from one another. They were isolated. They felt loss and guilt and frustration. They became self-centered and self-protective, bitter, angry, depressed, and dreadfully sad.

The problem of sin is far deeper than mere transgression of the law. And if we do not see the deeper problem, we will be left with a rather shallow understanding of our reconciliation in Christ, as well as of the very nature of our own existence and struggles. Sin is about losing our right minds, such that we are no longer able to see the goodness and love of the Father, and thus no longer free to live life in His unearthly assurance and blessing. We are left to live our lives in and out of fear and anxiety and dread. And those emotions create their own self-centered, self-protective world of hiding and brokenness, bitterness, frustration, and chaos.

Chapter 2

John and Charlie

Let me give you an illustration of what I mean by the alienation of our inner vision. When my friend John turned six, his Uncle Bob gave him a black and white border collie. Even today, John says it was the greatest present he has gotten. At the time he had no idea that a gift could be so good. He was thrilled and immediately named his new dog Charlie. Border collies, of course, are smart dogs, and the ones that I have known are capable of something very much akin to love. On this day, it was love at first sight. Charlie took to John like a martin to a gourd, and John's heart instantly bonded to Charlie's. From the first moment, John and Charlie were inseparable. Whether squirrel hunting or walking through the woods, swimming in the creek or playing baseball, or just sitting on the back porch shelling peas, if John was there, so was Charlie.

Charlie seemed the happiest dog on earth, full of life, loyal, present and poised for action, and ever ready to protect John. It was unthinkable for John to leave Charlie, except for Sunday morning church. Every evening, as a matter of ritual, John would reach down beside his bed and rub Charlie's ears. Then he would fall asleep in the comfort of his presence.

But somewhere around John's twelfth birthday, Charlie died. John did not tell me how it happened, and I didn't ask, as I noticed tears in his eyes after all these years. He said that the day Charlie died he felt his heart rip in half. With rivers of tears falling from his eyes, John picked up Charlie's lifeless body, grabbed a shovel, and dug a hole in the ground out back. He managed to fashion a cross out of a split boat paddle and some frayed rope from an old tire swing. He buried Charlie and mumbled a prayer.

Trembling and broken, he walked back to the house and stood on the back porch sobbing. His loyal and constant friend was gone forever, never again to bark at cars or growl at raccoons in the moonlight, never again to race behind him on his bike or swim with him in the creek or wake him in the morning. John felt the cold, unbearable wind of loneliness sweep into his heart. He stood on the back porch crying for what seemed to be hours.

John's parents and brothers were in the house. He thinks his aunt and uncle were there as well, and maybe some other folks. Yet with all those people around, no one noticed what was happening. There John stood, all twelve years of him, his beloved Charlie dead and gone, and no one came outside to comfort him. There were no hugs, no shared tears, no promises of a new dog, not even a gentle reminder that there are horses in Heaven in the book of Revelation, so that maybe it was possible for Charlie and John to be together again one day. John stood there all alone in his pain.

As John relayed the stories of Charlie to me, he smiled through his tears, and then he turned to me and said, "Baxter, I learned that afternoon on the back porch that I do not matter. I am not valuable. My feelings do not count."

Charlie's death, and the indifference of those around John, opened the door for a dreadful thought to whisper into his soul: "I am not important." Of course, John, like all of us, had heard that whisper before, many times and in many ways. But on the day Charlie died, on the day John stood alone in the cosmos, the whisper became a *conclusion* somewhere within John's soul. It was no longer a faint *suggestion*; it was now a *belief.* And such a conclusion changed the way he saw himself. It reconfigured the default settings of his self-image. This conclusion, with the damaged self-image it gave him, became the unconscious lens through which John began to perceive and interpret the world and people around him. Like a giant projector, John's heart flashed its belief onto every face and event, every act and word and thought he encountered. Everywhere he looked, he saw confirmation of his secret conclusion—*I am not important.*

How hard is it to see the evil scouts of disappointment pitching their tents in the backyard of John's future? It is easy to see, isn't it, how John could spend the next thirty or so years proving that he *was* important? Can you not see John launching out in his hurt to do something somewhere that would demonstrate once and for all that he *was* valuable, that he *did* count, that his existence *did* matter? How could he not become a workaholic? Or perhaps you can see John moving the other way, with the unbearable pain of it all shutting him down. Is it too difficult to see John drinking his pain away, or at least trying? The hurt is intolerable. "I am not important" is not an intellectual theory; it has become a core belief. Its brutal pain, like a coiled snake, could strike at any moment. With his insides so tormented by the lie, what is John to do? Act like all is well? Pretend that he is just fine?

On Saturdays, John plays golf or hunts or fishes, yet he seems unaware of what it means to *play*. Is that so strange? Is it odd that John has trouble accepting compliments, that he looks down when someone praises his work, his professionalism, or his creativity? He desperately craves affirmation, but how could he possibly hear it when it comes? Somewhere in the dark caverns of his soul, John *believes* that he is not important, and thus that compliments toward him, whatever else they could be, could not be the real truth—and neither could love, whether from his wife or his daughter or a friend.

With "I am not acceptable" so rooted in his soul, John is primed to see rejection everywhere he looks, even in the greatest gift. Living with a hair trigger in his soul, the slightest hint of indifference sends the old pain shooting through his heart, and off he goes running, hiding, withdrawing. Think of John's wife. How could she understand? Would she not feel constant pressure from John's pain, pressure to do something, to be something for John? Surely she would try—with all her heart she would try—to get things right, to crack the code, to manage his demanding, inner world, to keep things in balance. But it would never work. How could she heal this wounded little boy of a husband? No matter what she did, it could never be enough, never be right. And wouldn't John perceive her best efforts as another proof of his dreadful conclusion? Think about it. When we reach out to others isn't there a clear assumption that we think they need help?

How long could this go on before she would exhaust herself? How long could she walk on eggshells, tiptoeing around his hypersensitivity? How long could she live with John's absence as he chases a new salvation, or as he hides in the bottle? With "I am not important" running through his veins, can't you see John leaving a trail of wreckage behind him as the pain drives him to save himself, as his fear closes his heart and turns him into a self-centered parasite of a man?

The problem of sin is not merely that John did wrong things, although he did, and it is not difficult to see why. The problem of sin is that John's inner vision came to be terribly skewed, *and* this skewed inner vision then colored the way John saw himself and everything in his life, which in turn shaped the way he related or did not relate to the world around him.

Chapter 3

Stephanie and Her Dad

John's internal struggles are not so strange to us. They are all too human and familiar. Each of us, if we are honest, can see how we left our childhood with exit wounds that marred our sense of well-being. And each of us, if we are awake, can see how those wounds have created difficulty in our adult relationships. Our sense of self is critical to how we perceive the world and people around us. Let me relay another story to highlight how our self-perception, for good or ill, dominates our relationships.

Stephanie was a young girl in average America. Her parents worked hard, providing what the world around them considered important. All in all, she was as normal as sunshine. But there was more going on behind the scenes than meets the eye. Stephanie grew up under the harassment of an abusive father. He was not a bad man, and he was certainly not physically abusive. He was just a constant critic, as incapable of being pleased as he was of affirming others. Don't get me wrong. Stephanie's dad provided exceptionally for his family. In terms of material provisions, he was a success story in the American dream. He grew up in difficult times and he worked hard to make it. And he did. He had the house, the cars, and the picket fence to prove it. But on a personal level he was as absent as a robot, and as hypercritical as a Pharisee.

Stephanie loved her dad. In her eyes, he hung the moon. But instinctively she knew she had been dealt a bad hand. Over the years she came to feel that she could never quite get it right. She tried—with all her heart she tried. But to no avail. From her hair to her clothes, from her grades and her room to her tastes and her friends, she could never quite measure up. Sometimes her dad was straightforward in his criticism, but for the most part he was simply indifferent, cold, detached—emotionally absent. She always felt as though he was watching. His indifferent, yet ever—critical spirit seemed to haunt every room in the house, as if he was always there with his invisible ledger, passing judgment.

Neglect and non-affirmation can be as devastating as outright condemnation. The message is the same, although it has a different face. For Stephanie, her father's emotional absence and judgmental spirit steadily took their toll. Day by day, it was slowly etched into her mind that she was unacceptable.

On a cold Saturday morning, the ongoing message was forever sealed as brutal truth. Stephanie had waited for nearly a week for her report card. She watched through the window for the postman to come. After an hour she gave up, glancing around the room for something to do. She was biting her fingernails when she heard brakes squeal out front. She ran back to the window and saw the postman putting mail in their box. In a flash she was out the door. Opening the box, her longed-for letter was right on top, as if the postman knew. She ripped open the envelope. Seconds later, tears filled her eyes as she saw straight A's in the far right column. She had done it! She had worked so hard—and pulled it off. Thrilled, she ran inside shouting "Daddy, Daddy! I got all 'A's."

He was sitting in his chair, drinking coffee and reading the newspaper. She knew the unstated rule, "Do not disturb Daddy," but she couldn't help it. She stood staring at the newspaper between them, hoping against hope that he would at least put the paper down and acknowledge her and her achievement. But there was no response. Not a glance. Not a sigh. Not even a nod. "Daddy, I got all 'A's," she repeated, as the years of disappointment emptied her words of hope. Nothing. Holding her tears, she turned toward her room. Her dad sipped his coffee and muttered, *"You should have."*

Years of neglect finally burned their point into Stephanie's heart. It was a simple moment, and a simple statement—perhaps even of fact. Her dad was probably just reading the paper. In itself, *"You should have"* is not such a powerful or necessarily damaging statement. But given the terrible absence, it was an exclamation point at the end of a long hurt. The neglect, the indifference, the criticism, the singular lack of praise, the hurt, the loneliness, and the tears all funneled into those three words. The message was loud and clear. *"I do not measure up, and never will. I am not good enough. It is not okay to be me."*

The truth is, Stephanie is beautiful and talented and smart, but that is not the message she heard in her early life. Somewhere deep inside, she, like John, reached the conclusion that she was unacceptable. It was not an abstract conclusion based on a momentary affliction. It was the *period* at the end of a clear and repeated sentence. It was real, as real as her own heartbeat. She was worthless. "Wake up and smell the skunk. *Something is wrong with me.*"

Such a dreadful conclusion is unbearable, stirring as it does the most profound pain within the human soul. Who can cope with such pain? If we are made for our Father's affirmation, then rejection by our earthly dad cuts us to the quick. Stephanie, like most of us, had no real option but to bury it all in some secret corner and go on with her life. It never crossed her mind that she would carry the fearful pain within her, and that her father's ledger and its verdict and its emotional terror would always be there, hiding like a pack of coyotes, ready to pounce for the kill.

Somehow the deep fears of our buried wounds have a knack for attaching themselves to present situations, to events or smells, to music or certain noises or sights, even to the people we love and expressions on their faces. As a picture can paint a thousand words, a single look or sigh or newspaper can jab the raw nerve of our buried hurt, sending our insides reeling. At any moment, and for no apparent reason, an invisible war of pain could erupt within Stephanie's heart.

What was she to do? How could she cope? In time, she, like John, and many of us, unwittingly signed up for the game of self-justification. It was not clear at the moment, but looking back it is obvious that Stephanie set out on that Saturday to prove to herself that she *was* valuable. Come hell or high water, she would win. She had to win. Worthlessness is too profound to bear. The demons had to be silenced, and she had to feel good about herself. In her mind's eye, Stephanie chose to be *nice*. Inside she was brokenhearted. But if she could be nice, then she would be valuable, acceptable, and not worthless, and the demons would go away.

What Stephanie didn't know that she didn't know was that the game she joined would consume her, sabotaging her relationships and her dreams for life. The conclusion that she was worthless and the pursuit of imaginary niceness would give birth to another game: pretending. This unholy trinity—the sense of worthlessness, the striving for niceness, and pretending all is well—inevitably steals all vestiges of freedom to be a real person in relationship. Stephanie was trapped in her own conclusion, and did not even know it.

Life for Stephaine has become a stage. As long as people around her think she is nice, she feels good about herself. So she stays busy for others, or with important things that look like the nice, perfect life.

The game Stephanie plays is exhausting and deadly. She is driven by her conclusion to prove to the invisible, ubiquitous "they" somewhere out there that she is nice. She has many friends, but her relationships are only a thimble deep. No one can be allowed into the dressing room of her soul. Holding the world at arm's length, she whispers to herself, *"I am fine, there is nothing wrong with me. Can't you see how nice I am?"* How difficult it is to see the "Do not disturb" necklace around her neck, even while she wears herself out for others, reads her Bible, and earnestly prays for the lost.

Let's say she marries a man who worships the ground she walks on. In his eyes, Stephanie is the most beautiful person he has ever known. He adores her and affirms her constantly, but how could she possibly see his affirmation for what it is, let alone return it and share its joy? His love bounces off the stratosphere of her soul. She cannot receive it. She cannot believe it. Her wound and her way of being simply will not allow her to take his love seriously.

What if her husband becomes one of those strange points of attachment? What if through his sighs, or frowns, or criticism, or even through his smile, or care, her fearful wound is touched? What if she hears the old whisper, "I am not valuable, not loveable, not worthy," and feels its terrible pain when her husband struggles, or reads the newspaper, or even when he brings her flowers for no reason other than that he loves her?

How long will it take before her husband begins to think that the woman he loves is nice, but cold, detached—emotionally unavailable? Outside, she is on the go, exhausting herself for others. Inside, like a young girl in a woman's body, she is afraid, hesitant, and cautious, unable to risk being known, yet always looking the part. What is he to think? How could he not be dazed and confused?

She says she loves him, but she is so busy being nice she has no time to be known, not to mention time to receive his love and return his passion. What man could feel the pain of her hiding and absence and not take them personally? *Imagine if Stephanie were married to John.*

Stephanie's dreadful conclusion has become something of a self-fulfilling prophecy. Perfect and nice, but absent and unknowable, her game has thoroughly sabotaged a good relationship, all the while convincing her that she is whole and complete, in need of nothing. Reaping what she has perceived—and misperceived—she steadfastly evades the pain of looking at herself, while her marriage dies on the vine. What is left but to gather her friends to confirm her niceness and pity her great misfortune?

What sad and lonely scenarios. The rippling childhood traumas of John and Stephanie bring to the surface the fact that we all have deep beliefs about ourselves, and that those beliefs shape the way we perceive and relate to others. For good or ill, we all project our inner vision onto the world and people around us, often with devastating consequences. The critical question is, How in the world do we get around our own conclusions? How can we find new eyes and see the truth that is beyond our wounded perception? Why would John or Stephanie ever suspect that they had a problem? And even if they did, how could they begin to step outside their own way of seeing things?

What about the rest of us? Why would we even want new eyes, when the one thing we know for sure is that our vantage point is the obvious truth? It is inconceivable to us that *we* could be wrong—wrong about ourselves, wrong about others, wrong about life. And even if we thought there might be a problem with *us,* how in the world can a blind man give himself sight? How can we step outside our own wrong-headed perception and see things as they are, when our own perception determines what we see and how we see them? How do we get around our own baggage? How do we have real relationships, when our own marred vision shapes our perception of people themselves? We don't even know we have a problem.

The catastrophe of sin lies right here. Like John and Stephanie, we all bring our baggage and misperception into our relationships—and not just into our relationships with one another and with the creation, but—most critically—into our relationship with God. Without even knowing it, we impose our own thoughts upon God. As someone once said, "God created us in his own image, and we have been returning the favor ever since." As surely as John and Stephanie interpreted their world through their brokenness, so we interpret God through ours. The god we believe in is the product of our wounds. How will we ever see the face of the Father? How can we know who He is and what He is actually like, when we inevitably perceive Him through our alienated vision? How can we possibly believe in the Father's endless love when we project our own hurt and instability onto his heart? Where does that leave us? Without knowing the Father's love, how can we possibly avoid living in the disastrous anxiety and hopelessness of our secret mantra, "I am not acceptable?"

We can feel the hurt in John and Stephanie. We can see their blinding wounds and the life-canceling, relationship-destroying power of those wounds: The problem of sin is that we are in the same boat; in looking at them, we are looking at ourselves. *"No one knows the Father…"*

Chapter 4

Adam and Eve

Let me give you another picture. The Bible tells us in Genesis 3 that Adam and Eve *hid* in the bushes from the presence of the Lord. The obvious question is, Why? Why were they hiding? Clearly they were afraid, but afraid of what? Of course, their hiding comes on the heels of their outright disobedience, and most people would assume that they were afraid of God's punishment. But then again, how could Adam and Eve stand *in the garden,* the recipients of such astonishing blessing, and be afraid of *the Lord*? Had God changed? Had the Lord, who created Adam and Eve out of sheer grace and love and poured such astounding blessing upon them, suddenly done an about face? Had he ceased to love? Did the Lord transform himself from an eager and lavish philanthropist into a quick-tempered judge? Unlike John and Stephanie, Adam and Eve had no history of disappointment or hurt. There is no record of divine indifference or neglect, and certainly not of rejection and abuse. There is only astonishing and lavish blessing. So why would they suspect that the Lord would hurt them?

Surely Adam's disobedience did not alter the being of God. *Or perhaps it did.* Perhaps God did change, abruptly and radically so—not in reality of course, but in Adam's mind. Could it be that Adam's pain— the pain of his own unfaithfulness—altered his mind? Could it be that Adam's infidelity reconfigured his default settings? Could it be that his failure changed his understanding, his inner vision, his perception of himself, his world and others, but most importantly, the way he saw the face of God? Could it be that Adam projected his own brokenness onto God's face? Could it be that he tarred the Father's face with the brush of his own angst? Perhaps Adam took a paintbrush, dipped it into the cesspool of his own double-mindedness and guilt, and painted an entirely new picture of god with it. And perhaps it was this god, created by his own darkened imagination—not the Lord—that he feared, and from whom he hid.

How could Adam change God? How could human action of any kind change the being of God? Is the character of God so fickle, so unstable, as to be dependent upon us, or upon what we do or do not do? As my friend Gary Arinder says, "God does not walk around with a thermometer in His hands taking our temperature to see how He feels about Himself or about us." God is God, the same now as always, steadfast in love, unbending in faithfulness, eager and determined to bless and share life, overflowing in grace and mercy and fellowship as Father, Son, and Spirit. What changed in the relationship was not God, but Adam, and he now projected his pain onto God, thereby creating an entirely mythological deity, a figment of his own baggage. But this figment was nevertheless frighteningly real *to Adam.*

Standing before this mythological god, this projection, Adam was scared to death. How could he not be? He believed himself to be standing guilty before a divine being who was as unstable as he. Sheer terror struck his soul. For in his fallen mind, he was staring down the gun barrel of utter rejection. In his mythology, he stood a hair's breadth from abandonment and the abyss of non-being.[3]

This is the problem of sin. The impossible has happened: The truth about the Father is eclipsed. The unforgettable love of the triune God is now forgotten, so forgotten that it is now *inconceivable.* A profound blindness has taken over Adam's mind. He cannot see the Father's face. There is now a terrible incongruence between the being and character of God as Father, Son, and Spirit and the divine being Adam *perceives* and *believes* God to be. And for Adam, and indeed for all of us, the god of our imaginations is the only way God can be. Any other god makes no sense to us.

From this moment, the Father's face will be forever tarred with an alien brush, and His heart, His beauty, His goodness, will be misunderstood. Our darkened imagination will recreate the Father's character in its own image. Our shame will disfigure the Father's heart. The projections of our fear will rewrite the rules of His care. He will continue to bless us beyond our wildest dreams, but in our mythology we will see His gifts and hear "I am not acceptable" confirmed. The very presence of the Lord in love and grace and fellowship will be translated through the fallen mind and perceived as the presence of One who is at best cold, detached and indifferent, and at worst the great critic, the judge quick

---

[3] The phrase "the abyss of non-being" is from Dr. Bruce Wauchope's lecture: "The Gospel and Mental Health." This lecture is available at <www.perichoresis.org>.

to condemn, whose judgmental, watching spirit haunts every room in the universe.

The human race is lost in the most terrible darkness—the darkness of its own fallen mind, the darkness of wrong belief and unfaithfulness, of anxiety and projection and misperception. Tragically, the fallen mind is consistent. It never fails. Its dark and anxious imagination creates a false deity, the proof of which it sees everywhere it looks. And this god is very, very real to us, so real that it has become quite "natural" to us, the most obvious thing in the world, the unquestionable truth about divinity, through which we misperceive the heart of the Father without even knowing it.

Out of this world of darkness we live and act and hurt one another. The story of Adam and Eve demonstrates that the problem of our blindness does not originate with our parents, but is far deeper. Yet the darkness of our parents and culture, and even of our churches, confirms and exacerbates the deeper issues of our marred vision of the Father.

It would be far easier if sin were merely a legal matter, for then God could arrange a legal sacrifice to cover our sins and all would be well. But such a view, while quite consistent with the mythology of the fallen mind and its projections, fails to answer the fundamental problem: What kind of forgiving God could be satisfied with having the guilty legally clean, yet so trapped in their wrong-headedness and anxiety that they cannot possibly receive His forgiveness and live in His joy? What kind of reconciliation leaves us in our darkness, hiding in the fear of our mythological deity, utterly blind to the Father's heart and lost to the freedom of His embrace? What kind of reconciliation leaves us at the mercy of generational, cultural, and ecclesiastical darkness, with no way to perceive the love of the Father?

I saw an interview once with a man whose daughter had been murdered. The murderer had been caught and tried, and the court had issued the death sentence. The interviewer, scurrying to be first in line to speak with the father, stuck the microphone in his face, and asked, "Do you feel that justice is at last being served?" Staring a hole straight through the poor interviewer, the father shot back, "There can never be justice until I get *my daughter back.*"

Jesus' Father is not and never will be satisfied with mere forgiveness or legal reconciliation. How could He be? Such a "forgiveness" and "reconciliation" would leave us lost to His heart and hiding from Him in our fear. Such a reconciliation would leave John trapped in his isolation, and Stephanie bound to live with a god made in the image of her dad. The truth is, however, that Jesus' Father will not rest until His forgiveness has cut a swath into our pain, until His forgiveness is known in our darkness, received and believed, and issues forth in the restoration of *our* fellowship with Him and our forgiveness of others.

Questions for Reflection

(1) Describe how John *felt* as he stood on the back porch. What are the times in your life when you felt the same ways? Do these feelings sometimes surface again for no apparent reason?

(2) Do you think you have reached a secret conclusion about yourself? What is it? What has it proved to you? Is there a relationship between your secret conclusion, your feelings, and your vision of God?

(3) If you had only one word to describe God, what would it be? Why?

(4) List the main people, words, and events that have most shaped your vision of God. How has your view of God changed over the years? What contributed to the change?

(5) What about our Father makes you most proud?

(6) Have you ever felt the Father say to you, "Well done?" If you could overhear the Father, Son, and Spirit talking about you, what would you hear? What about you delights our Father?

(7) In what ways do you "tar the Father's face with the brush of your own angst?" How do you do the same with your husband or wife or friends?

(8) How do you respond when you feel the disappointment of others? How do you protect yourself from the hurt of this disappointment? What do you do to fix the problem?

(9) How have your past hurts attached themselves to present situations or people or events? What do you do when you are sad?

(10) What do you pray for most earnestly? Why? In what ways has the Lord answered your prayer? Could He be answering in ways that you cannot see?

(11) What do you think of the statement, "We are designed to be quickened with life through spiritual knowledge of the Father's heart, and then for this life to overflow in other-centered love to others and into all creation?"

Part 2

Incarnation and Reconciliation

Chapter 5

He Knows

Reconciliation is not about Jesus suffering punishment so that the invisible, faceless and nameless god up there somewhere can forgive us. It is about the Father's forgiveness in action, entering into our estrangement and its hell, and penetrating the fundamental problem of sin. As James Torrance would say, "The Father does not have to be conditioned into being gracious." There is no sense in which He needs to be coerced in order to forgive. Forgiveness is first, overflowing out of the way in which the Father, Son and Spirit love one another. From this forgiveness arises passion for it to be known and received.

Reconciliation began when the Father saw that His children could not see His heart, the Son realized that we could not receive his Father's love, and the Spirit saw the joy of fellowship with the Father vanish from our lives. Reconciliation is about the Father sending His own Son into our darkness. It is about the Son identifying with us, seeing our god, feeling our fear, experiencing our brokenness. Reconciliation is about the Spirit bridging the horrible gap between the Father's heart and our blindness, as Jesus embraced it in his own being. It is the suffering of the triune God, righting the doomed ship of our fallen minds, until we know the Father with Jesus in the fellowship of the Spirit.

Reconciliation is the Father's forgiveness determined to become flesh, determined to incarnate itself into our fallen existence in order to undo our alienation. It is the relationship, the fellowship and communion of the Father, Son, and Spirit stepping into our blindness and mythology, into the cesspool of our trauma and wounds, so that human perception can be thoroughly converted and the Father's love can be truly known and experienced. The purpose, the aim, the object of reconciliation is not to change God, but to bring *us* into communion with the Father, so that we could know Him and His lavish heart and live life in the freedom of His embrace.

But how do you penetrate human wrong-headedness? How can the forgiving Father even begin to reach *us* in our darkness? How can He possibly cross the frontiers of our alienation and baggage and bring us to know His heart? Revelation is the obvious answer, but what good is revelation without the healing of our minds? What good is a beautiful painting if we have wrong eyes? Without the conversion of the fallen mind, our "internal processor" remains broken. So we do not have the capacity to receive the revelation and know the Father. What the Father *says* is one thing, what we *hear* is quite another. The revelation of the Father to us, irrespective of how powerful and clear and inerrant it is from His side, is always perceived through our mental baggage, through our alien and alienating vision, and that revelation is therefore always skewed by our minds.

The fallen mind is a misreading machine. But it is really worse than that. We not only misread the communication of the Father; we take our misreading and build our own vision of god with it. It is inescapable. Out of the very truth revealed to us, our projections manufacture an utterly foreign god. And then, we misuse the word of God itself to prove our own darkened notions of divine being. Revelation itself thus becomes more grist for our mythological mill—divinely sanctioned proof that our conception of god is the truth. We are caught in a hermeneutical nightmare and don't even know it. And the nightmare is so "natural" to us, we could never entertain even a doubt about its vision of god. Any other vision of god is inconceivable. For the one unquestionable absolute in the universe of our minds is that our notion of god could not possibly be wrong.

How will we ever escape the quagmire of our own fallen minds? How will humanity ever break out of the nightmare and come to know the true Father? How will we ever see the Father as He truly is, and thus begin to live in the assurance and freedom and joy of His embrace? Who can know the Father?

The human plight is truly hopeless. We have only one mind, and it is thoroughly alien to the truth. There is therefore no escape from our own twisted self-referential incoherence. Unable to step out of our own fallen minds, we cannot push our mythological projection to the side and get a true vision of the Father's heart. And even if we could, we would never believe it as the truth. It would be too incredible, too foreign, too strange, too good to accept. Face to face with the outright impossibility of our knowing the Father, and the misery-producing doom of living life in the absence of His unearthly assurance, we are poised to appreciate the doctrine of the trinity and the shocking reality of the incarnation of the Father's eternal Son.

The doctrine of the trinity means that, strictly speaking, God is not alone. Within the being of God there is relationship—three persons united in mutual love and communion without loss of personal distinctness. The relationship of the Father, Son, and Spirit is a rich and unclouded fellowship that is so deep and true, so open and close, fired by such pure love, that we are driven with historic Christianity to say they are *one*. Anything less than "one" betrays the very depth and closeness of their relationship. Yet the Father does not become the Son or Spirit and the Son and Spirit do not become one another or the Father. This is a relationship of oneness, yet not of absorption. This is a relationship of thoroughgoing communion in mutual self-giving love, in which the Father, Son, and Spirit have such a profound freedom to know and be known that they share all things together without losing themselves in enmeshment.

The reality of the trinitarian life of God means there is hope for the human race trapped in its alien and alienating vision. The hermeneutical nightmare is not the end of the story. For there is one who truly knows the Father and shares all things with Him in the fellowship of the Spirit. There is one whose default settings are not alien to the Father's heart, one who knows the Father as He is, one who sees His face and experiences His lavish love. There is one who believes. *Imagine:* What if this one entered into our darkness? What if this Son became human? What if this Son stepped into the gnarled and twisted world of the fallen Adamic mind?

I do not mean, "What if the Son became human in order to reveal the Father to us?" Such revelation is, of course, absolutely critical, but in itself revelation alone does not solve the problem. For we are blind and cannot receive it. And worse, as we have seen, our twisted minds turn the revelation of the Father into proof of our false god. But what if the Father's Son stepped into Adam's skin, put on Adam's fallen eyes and *received* the revelation of the Father for us? And what if he used our twisted darkness to do so?

Chapter 6

The Shocker

This, of course, is exactly what happened in the shocking reality of the incarnation. The eternal Son of the Father became flesh. He entered into our human existence, into the far country of our profound blindness. Jesus Christ did not come to change God. He came to identify with us, to stand on our side of the mess, to see what we see in our blindness and shame. He did not come to camp out on the frontiers of our great darkness and shout across the chasm. He came to experience the hell of Adam's alien vision, and thus to establish a bridgehead between his communion with his Father and the human race in its tragic mythology.

The miracle of the incarnation is that the Son of the Father stepped not only into human existence in some abstract sense, but into the quagmire of Adam's fallen mind—into his skewed vision and the traumatic existence of his mythology. As the gospel teaches, the Word became not only human, but *flesh* (John 1:14). Jesus became John sobbing on the back porch, Stephanie seeing out of wounded eyes. He stood in our place, in our pitiful darkness, and feeling our shame, found his way inside our damaged, projecting, mythological deity-creating self-image. Whatever it was that Adam painted onto the Father's face, and whatever it was that he felt when he did so, Jesus Christ saw and felt, and he saw it and felt it with the same intensity and reality as Adam.[4]

The eternal Son of the Father truly entered the fallen world—and he did not come with a cloaking device to shield him from our suffering. He came to experience our tragedy for himself. So he embraced the world where his Father's face has been tarred with the brush of human pain, the mythological world where the Father's eyes have been painted

---

[4] For a more complete treatment of the work of Christ, see C. Baxter Kruger, *Jesus and the Undoing of Adam* (Jackson: Perichoresis Press, 2003) and *The Great Dance* (Jackson: Perichoresis Press, 2000; Vancouver: Regent College Publishing, 2005).

with indifference and disgust, judgment and rejection. Refusing to watch from a safe distance, the Father's Son invaded our darkness and alienation, where our fallen minds have created a pagan god so real to us that it would never cross our minds to question its character, and where we sabotage our lives in living out of this vision in self-protecting fear, hiding, and brokenness.

"My God, My God, why have You forsaken Me?"[5] Who has cried this cry? Is this not the cry of Adam, blind and trembling in the bushes? Is this not the bone-chilling conclusion of John on the back porch and the terrible verdict of Stephanie's childhood? Is this not the unspeakable fear of every human heart trapped in the great darkness, with no true vision of the Father? And is this not the terrifying hell that Jesus embraced, the withering, appalling, gut-wrenching pain of our perceived rejection by god?

Jesus saw Adam's god, the unstable, quick-tempered judge, eagerly watching every move from the infinite distance of a disapproving heart. He saw this god with Adam's eyes. Under the shame of our angst-ridden imaginations, mocked by the endless misperception of the self-righteous and the ridicule of the all-seeing religious eye, Jesus met Adam's god, our god, the god of the fallen mind. He identified with us. He heard the haunting, harassing whisper, "I am not acceptable, not good enough, not important," feeling the bitter curse of its judgment. With the leaves of the garden rustling the rumor of our failure, he stared into the terrifying shadows of rejection and abandonment. Clothed in Adamic humanity, pierced with the brutal loneliness of universal rejection, he stood speechless before the refrain of the lie: *"I am not acceptable. I am not good enough. I am separated from God—the proof is everywhere."*

From the cradle to the grave, Jesus Christ was one of us, seeing what we see, feeling what we feel, knowing what we know, and even more. Baptized in the terrible insecurity of our cloud of unknowing, afflicted with our conscience, pestered by the whisper of evil—and damned by his own people—Jesus experienced what we never dare allow ourselves to face. Standing alone before absolute rejection, he squared off against the invisible arms of non-being as they snatched for his seemingly untethered soul.

---

[5] Psalm 22:1; Matthew 27:46. For a more extended discussion of this cry from Jesus on the cross, see C. Baxter Kruger, *Jesus and the Undoing of Adam* (Jackson: Perichoresis Press, 2003), pp. 58ff.

Chapter 7

He Found the Father

But—and the existence and destiny of the universe hang on this *but*—
Jesus Christ refused to believe a word of it. Face to face with Adam's
god, feeling the hair rise on the back of Adam's neck, crushed under the
weight of the crowd's rejection, Jesus steadfastly refused to acknowledge this god or this world and its verdict, or this future, as real at
all. Stepping into the fallen world of Adam, he absolutely refused to
be "fallen" in it. The one who knows the Father embraced the gnarled
and twisted world of our darkness and pain, where the whisper of evil
and the fear of rejection, the threat of abandonment and cosmic loneliness, self-serving betrayal and the blindness of the crowd utterly rule
the human scene. There, Jesus—the good shepherd, accused of leading
the sheep astray; the anointed one, accused of being possessed by evil;
the Father's true Son mocked as a bastard and rejected—there, Jesus
took his stand. Against the whole world, he fought his way through the
trenches of our delusion, through the terrorizing jungles of our tragic
nightmare, through the sneering, hostile judgment of his own people,
to find his Father's face. Inside Adam's skin, peering through our wrong
eyes, seeing the unstable watcher, feeling the trauma of the world's
insanity, Jesus found his Father and His lavish embrace in the fellowship of the Spirit.

Reconciliation is not about changing God. It is about the Father's
Son entering the darkness and so suffering its pain that a personal rela-
tionship, a living union is formed between our tragic blindness and the
Father's heart.

The revelation of the Father's heart, so disfigured by the projections of anxious humanity, found a reconciling foothold in the fallen
mind assumed by the incarnate Son. He refused to believe in the god
of Adam. In the teeth of our wrong belief and projections, restless with
our anxiety and hopelessness, baptized with our insecurity, bearing the
pain of our panic-stricken souls, he incarnated his own knowledge of

the Father. Inside the hell of our fallen mind and the hell it makes of the world and relationships, the Son was steadfastly faithful to himself as the Father's Son. He believed. Standing alone and condemned, feeling the affliction of the whisper, experiencing the shame of the system's sneer, he fought through the darkness, the pain, the rejection, the veil of unknowing, the mythology and its trauma, and experienced his Father's love.

At every point, through fire and trial and tribulation, through condemnation and shame, through fears without and within, He broke through the great darkness into the knowledge of the Father. At every level of human despair, Jesus found his Father and the healing fellowship of His embrace in the Spirit. He loved the Father with all his heart, soul, mind, and strength. This is the miracle of the reconciling love of the Father in the incarnate life, death, resurrection, and ascension of His beloved Son. The one who knows the Father embraced our darkness, using our own bitter rejection of himself as the way to penetrate deeper and deeper into our estrangement.

How could this be? How could the eternally beloved Son of the Father truly enter into our blindness and fear and insecurity? How could *he* step into Adam's mythological world and take on our baggage and skewed vision? How could the Father's Son, who lives face to face with the Father Himself, assume Adam's fallen mind, riddled with its pagan god, its insecurities and pain, its fear of rejection, its self-centeredness and endless hiding? How could this Son suffer the condemnation of the world? Herein lies the paradox of the incarnation and the very meaning of reconciliation.

The incarnation of the Son of God means nothing short of the incarnation of the communion of the Father, Son, and Spirit, and it means the incarnation of the trinitarian fellowship precisely in the mythological world where our communion has been shattered with impossibility. The beloved Son lived out his own sonship, his own unbroken fellowship with his Father, inside our hell. The sheer beauty of his relationship with his Father exposed us all as empty, sad, and broken. His life in the Spirit revealed our religion to be dead. His goodness stripped away our pretense. We hated him for it. We rejected him and ridiculed his heart. We made him the scapegoat for all our ills.

"Crucify him! Crucify him!" (Mark 15:13–14; John 19:6) This is the universal verdict of the "natural" mind. For 33 years Jesus experienced our abuse. He experienced the venomous pain of our hostile indifference and rejection. He used this experience as the way of incarnation. He used it to "hammer out," as J. B. Torrance would say, his own knowledge

of the Father, "on the anvil" of our terrible brokenness. Clinging to his Father's love and to the witness of the Spirit, Jesus *suffered* the incarnation of the trinitarian communion into the hell of our alienated human existence. Instead of retaliating, instead of returning our anger and rejection with his own anger and rejection, Jesus embraced our enmity. He faced, felt and endured our anger. He experienced our rejection personally, and in doing so he established a real relationship between the trinitarian life he lives and the human race at its absolute worst.

Reconciliation is not a theoretical doctrine; it is not even news. Reconciliation is the relationship established between the triune God and the human race in Jesus through his own painful incarnation. In this impossible union between the Son who knows the Father and the human race so violently lost in the darkness lies the mystery of the incarnation and of reconciliation—and the hope of the human race.

There is one who knows the Father. There is one from our broken and twisted world of wrong belief and projecting fear who sees the Father's face and believes. There is one from our terrifying nightmare, one from the cold silence of the great darkness, one from the hell of human betrayal who knows the unearthly assurance of the Father's heart. The dark and traumatic and fallen world of Adam's mythology has been invaded and experienced, exposed and shattered in Jesus Christ. He knows the Father in the deepest recesses of our hell.

Chapter 8

What If

There was no rest in the Father's heart until one inside the pain of Adam's tragic darkness came to know the truth about Him and taste and feel and experience His passionate, unflinching love. This is why the Son of God became human. He came to know his Father and life in His embrace, as he has always known Him and experienced that life, but now from inside our pain and wounds and fear.

At this very hour, one from the hell of Adam's traumatizing mythology sits at the Father's right hand. He sees not through brokenness and baggage—he sees clearly, face to face with the Father Himself. And what does Jesus Christ see in the Father's eyes? What does he know? What does he feel? What does he experience?

Is it hopelessness? Is it fear? Is Jesus scared? Does Jesus feel that he sits beside a father who is cold, detached, and indifferent, whose disapproving heart watches every move he makes? Is the fundamental truth of the Father's heart toward His Son that of a judge? Does Jesus hear "I am not acceptable, not important, not of any value," whispering through the halls of heaven? Does he struggle, hoping against hope that the Ogre will have a good hair day and overlook his failures? Does he see the world's scoffing verdict reflected in the Father's face?

Think about it. Think about it long and hard. What does Jesus Christ experience at the Father's right hand? Are his knuckles white, grasping the spider's web as he dangles over the flames of hell? Is Jesus exhausted from hiding, from pretending, from keeping appearances up? Is he weary with the fear of it all, wondering if today the faceless, all-powerful potentate will finally leave him on the edge of the abyss, banished from His presence and abandoned forever?

Think of the incarnate Son right now, sitting at the Father's side. Can you not see *how* the Father *loves* His Son? Can you not see His sheer delight? Think of the Father's heart. Think of how He looks at His Son. What do you see in the Father's eyes? Think of how His words, His touch, His embrace, are filled with pride. "Thou art *My beloved Son,* in whom *My soul delights*" (Matthew 3:17; 17:5). What does Jesus know? What does Jesus experience in the Father's presence? Does the condemnation of the world carry weight at the Father's right hand? How could Jesus be afraid?

There is no whispering at the Father's side. There the shame of the blind is silenced and the darkness has no voice. Jesus is the apple of the Father's eye—and he knows it. In his Father's eyes he sees no hesitance or neutrality or indifference. His Father loves. Jesus knows no fear for today or tomorrow. Unearthly assurance baptizes every nook and cranny of Jesus' soul as he sees the Father's face in the fellowship of the Spirit. At his Father's right hand, looking into eyes filled with ancient love, the beloved Son knows the sheer hope and freedom of the Father's passionate embrace.

Now, what if this Son turned and shared himself and his mind with you? What if Jesus reached into his own soul, as it were, and took his own spiritual knowledge of the Father's heart and gave it to you, put it in your soul? What if he were able to penetrate our projections and share his own perception with us in our fallenness? This is where the gift Jesus gives to the human race is far greater than any religion. This is the stunning turn in the history of human existence.

The good news of Jesus Christ is not that at last we have an accurate religious manual to follow and a master leader to show us the way. And it is not that we finally have perfect information about God to learn. The gospel is about Jesus himself. He *knows* the Father. And the gospel is about the stunning fact that the Father's Son has established a real relationship with us in our darkness. And in this relationship, he is sharing with us—with the world—his own mind and knowing, his own communion with his Father, forever. What a gracious, merciful brother. He bears our sneers, suffers our hostility, and returns for them his own knowledge of the Father's heart.

Remember, we are wired to experience life in fellowship with the Father and in soul knowledge of His delight. But we have only one mind, and it is utterly blind to the Father. We cannot push the weeds of our fallenness to the side and see the Father's heart. Left to ourselves, we have no option but to live in our own broken notions of god and the hell they create. We are imprisoned in the dungeon of our mythology where our god cannot be trusted, and the one thing we know for sure is that we are not good enough, not acceptable, not important. But what if Jesus Christ has found his way into our world? What if he could step into our hurt, our anger and rejection? What if he could penetrate our denial and share his own knowledge of the Father's heart with us? What if he could take what he knows of the Father and walk right into John's pain as he stood trembling on the back porch? What if he could reach into Stephanie's soul? What if Jesus could steal behind the watchful dragons of our mythology and share himself with us?[6]

Herein lies the very heart of the gospel of Jesus Christ, and of forgiveness itself. He has known the Father from all eternity, and he also knows the Father from inside our tragic nightmare. The gospel is the news that this Jesus is now sharing *himself* with you and me, and indeed with the world—*inside our darkness.* That is the only reason there is any sanity in our world at all.

Jesus knows the trauma of being human in a fallen world. He walked into the darkness, where we cower, where we fight to pretend all is right, where we busy ourselves to avoid hearing, where we frantically grasp at anything to find relief—and where we condemn any hint of our exposure. In the place where we can find no hope, no solace, where we see no possibility of tomorrow, he faced the sleepless demons and their accusing shadows. Staring into the lifeless eyes of the abyss, Jesus threw himself headlong into the jaws of our greatest fear. Free-falling in the darkness of Adam's mind, Jesus found the unfailing arms of His Father.

Is there a place in our darkness that does not bear his footprints? Where could we go that he has not been? What pain could we suffer that he has not known, and learned the hope of his Father's love within? Think this through. Is there a wound so deep that it cannot be reached by Jesus with his knowledge of the Father? Is there an abuse so traumatic, a betrayal so brutal, a rejection so personal, as to be beyond the experience of Jesus Christ himself and his healing light?

Are we unreachable in our brokenness? Is our darkness impenetrable? Is there a corner of the abyss of non-being that Jesus overlooked? What is there about our hell that is beyond Jesus Christ? What whisper has he not heard? What shame, what injustice, what rejection, what condemnation has he not felt? Is there a single leaf in our broken and mythological world that Jesus Christ has left unturned? Through living, through fire and trial, through hands-on experience of the great

---

[6] The imagery of "watchful dragons" comes from C. S. Lewis' essay, "Sometimes Fairy Stories Say Best What's to Be Said," in *On Stories and Other Essays on Literature,* edited by Walter Hooper (New York: Harcourt Brace & Company, 1982), p. 47. I am grateful to Cary Stockett for sharing the image with me.

darkness, through suffering the abusive condemnation of the human race, through finding his Father in the hell of the human plight, Jesus has received the love of the Father into the fallen Adamic mind. He has received the anointing of the Spirit into every form of human brokenness. Is Jesus not now the most seasoned prophet in the universe? Does he not know how to minister the Father's heart to us where we are? Is he not able to share his Spirit with us in the darkest corners of our fear?

The gospel is the news that Jesus became what we are, and within our fear-twisted world of whispers, of darkness and rejection, he fought his way forward into the vision of the Father's heart. *He knows the Father.* With Adam's eyes, he sees the Father's face and knows the unearthly assurance of His embrace, and the sheer joy of His heart. The unspeakable communion of the Father, Son, and Spirit has pitched its tent inside our hell itself—forever. But that is only the beginning of the gospel. For this Jesus, in his stunning grace, is now sharing what he knows with us. He is not huddling in the corner of the tent with his Father. Our hell has become his heaven. The darkness has become his light. He is free to be himself as the Father's Son and the anointed one in our world of illusion. "The light shines in the darkness" (John 1:5). "Take courage; I have overcome the cosmos" (John 16:33).

Is this a polite theological dream? Is this another chapter of our religious romanticism? Could God be this good? Could we be so wrong? What if it is so? What if Jesus is this good? What if he is already out of the tent? What if he has already stolen behind the watchful dragons? What if he is not waiting for us to clean up our acts and invite him into our world? What if he has already accepted us as we are, already met us in our shattered lives? What if he is already walking through our fallen minds, already sharing himself with us? Could it be that there is far more going on in our lives than we ever dared dream? Could it be that we are now included in his knowledge of the Father?

The gospel is not the news that you can be involved with Jesus, if only you get your religion right. The gospel is not news of what *can be* at all. It is news of what *is.* It is the news that you *are* involved. It is not a dream. Through bearing our rejection, Jesus has access to us in our darkness. Indeed, he used our rejection to establish a relationship with us at our very worst. The stunning truth is that Jesus exists in union with his Father and the Spirit, *and with us in our darkness.* He has included us in his world, in his life and communion with his Father, in his anointing with the Spirit. He is sharing his own heart, his own knowledge of the Father, his own assurance and hope and joy with us all. He is putting his communion with his Father inside our own endarkened souls.

It is not a question of whether or not we are worthy of such a gift or whether or not we have earned his grace. It is a question of his abounding love and of his prophetic skill—born in the crucible of our blindness and abuse—to reach us in our darkness. He is an expert at knowing his Father in our hell. He accepts us and meets us where we are, and he is sharing himself with us in our brokenness and sin.

Do you know who you are and what is going on in your life? Do you know that you are the one Jesus loves, you are the one the Father has determined to come to know His heart? It is not about you inviting Jesus into your life; it is about Jesus already including you in his. Through his suffering he has forged a living union between his communion with his Father and you in your darkness. Jesus dwells in your darkness. He is sharing himself with you now. He always has been and always will. He will never stop giving himself, his mind and heart and soul, to you. He is passionate about your coming to know his Father with him and living life in the freedom of the Spirit of adoption. This is the non-negotiable of the grace of the triune God.

Chapter 9

The Command of Belonging

We belong to the Father, Son and Spirit. We always have, and always will. It is this blessed fact, this truth that in Jesus Christ the Father has established an abiding relationship with us in the Spirit, that tells us who we are and why we are here. We have a beautiful life to live. We are included in the trinitarian life of God. It is ours forever, as much our life as it is the life of the Father, Son and Spirit. Our place at the Father's table is eternal, as eternal as Jesus' own relationship with his Father. This is the truth, the real world, the ways things are and forever will be.

Written into the truth, and into the knowledge of the Father's love that Jesus himself is sharing with you, is the command of faith: "Trust me. Dare to doubt your vision of god. Believe in my Father and His love." And with the command of faith is the summons of freedom: "Get up, stand on your feet, and live in the joy of my knowledge of the Father's heart."

Implicit in the truth, its command to faith, and its summons to freedom is a serious warning. For at every point we are free to deny the truth and cling to our own way of seeing. We are free to live in our own worlds and to impose our illusions upon others—or try. Such a non-relational world is utterly foreign to who we are, but we can live in this world, dooming ourselves to suffer the consequences of hanging onto our projecting fear and the god of our imaginations. But why? Why choose such a broken existence? Why choose the tragic and miserable hell of belonging to the trinitarian world and yet insisting on living in our own? Why oppose such a Father? Why resist Jesus?

The great irony is that it is Jesus Christ alone who enters into our dark worlds and walks with us in them. No other person truly can or will. He meets us in our fallen minds.

> I, the one who has been there, the one who understands
> your darkness, the one who has cried your cries, tasted your
> shame, felt your fears, the one who has seen your god and his
> rejection, I embrace you and take responsibility for finding
> a reconciling foothold in your fallen mind. As I walk into
> your alienation and share myself with you, my knowledge of
> the Father's heart commands you to rise and live. I will walk
> with you in your world of darkness. I will bear your scorn. I
> will jump with you into the abyss of non-being, so that you
> can know that it is not, and never has been, and never will be
> real at all, so that you can know that there is only the Father's
> embrace.

You can see now why the New Testament is so full of the summons to repent and believe in Jesus. We are so confused and lost in the darkness. But Jesus is sharing himself with us, and in so doing he commands us to a vast reinterpretation of our own existence. We are not rejected. We are not separated from God. The Father loves us with an endless love, and He has found us in His Son. This is what repentance is all about; it is a radical change of mind, a thoroughgoing reorientation of the way *we perceive* God Himself and His heart, of the way we perceive ourselves and others. Jesus shares his mind with us and commands us to put aside our own judgment. He is not asking us to be brainless or to give up our own minds—he is telling us that our default settings are dead wrong, and that they are killing us. In staggering grace, Jesus has made us part of his world and his life with his Father and Spirit. He is commanding us to see what he sees, to believe with him, to participate in his way of seeing his Father. He gives us his own faith and summons us to accept and live in it. He shares his own unearthly assurance with us and commands us to rest.

What will happen to us when our fallen minds are restructured by the faith and knowledge of Jesus Christ—when, as Paul says, "we all come to the unity of the faith and of the knowledge of the Son of God"? (Ephesians 4:13). What will happen to us when we know as we are known? (I Corinthians 13:12) What will happen to our relationships with one another, and with the whole creation, when Jesus' knowledge of the Father's heart has free reign in our souls? What will happen when he teaches us to be seasoned veterans in finding his Father's love in every twisted form of darkness?

Jesus crosses all the worlds of our unknowing and meets us in our mythology. He is not afraid of our darkness. He dwells there in the freedom of the Spirit. He shares his light and life and love with us. What will happen to you when Jesus proves himself the seasoned prophet, the true and faithful witness, when he finds his reconciling foothold in your darkness? What will happen to you when you say, "Amen, come, Lord Jesus?" What will happen to you as you give him permission to walk through the corridors of your soul with his peace and to restructure your default settings in his light?

Consider this prayer.

> Lord Jesus Christ, beloved, eternal, and faithful Son of the Father incarnate, thank you for sharing your knowledge of the Father's heart with me. Come into my darkness with your light. Search out my blindness and share your unearthly assurance with me in the place of my deepest fears. Find all my broken parts and bathe them with your Father's love. Send your Spirit to baptize my soul with your peace.

What will happen to us as we pray this prayer? What will happen to our god, to the mythological deity we fear? What will happen to our fear and our terrible insecurity, to our hiding, our hesitant spirit, to our greed and lust and lethargy? What will happen to our self-centeredness and broken relationships? Will chaos abound? Will we be destroyed? Of course not. We will have, we will taste, we will know, we will feel the unearthly assurance of Jesus Christ himself as he sits at the Father's right hand. In the place of our unspeakable fear and its debilitating fruit we will know the unutterable love of the Father, Son, and Spirit. And such soul knowledge will set us free to live life in the Father's embrace, and the life and relationship of the Father, Son, and Spirit will overflow into our relationships with one another and with all creation. The Son's knowledge of his Father in the Spirit will cover the earth as the waters cover the sea (Isaiah 11:9; Habbakuk 2:14).

Questions for Reflection

(1) Do you think that our Father forgave us before His Son became human? What is the difference between a "legal" and an "incarnational" view of reconciliation?

(2) What is your most frequent feeling when you think about God? Why is it so hard to feel the Father's love?

(3) Why did Jesus suffer? Who caused his suffering? Did he suffer from the Father? What is hell, and how did Jesus experience it?

(4) Is there part of the Father that Jesus hides from us?

(5) How did Jesus use our rejection of him to work out reconciliation?

(6) What do you make of this statement: "Reconciliation is not about changing God. It is about the Father's Son entering the darkness, and so suffering its pain that a personal relationship, a living union is formed between our tragic blindness and the Father's heart."

(7) Why do you think Jesus was so widely rejected?

(8) What did Jesus have that enabled him to endure the mocking and ridicule of the religious leaders of his day?

(9) What would change in your life if you knew the Father as Jesus does? What would change in the Church?

(10) Is there something about you or others that you think is beyond the healing light of Jesus? Is your sorrow unreachable?

(11) What are the personal and relational consequences of living in our own worlds and hanging onto the god of our imaginations?

(12) What is the heart of the gospel?

(13) What would have to change in your thinking if the Trinity were not the truth about God?

Part 3

The Crisis

Chapter 10

The Edge of Good News

Sharing in Jesus' relationship with his Father is as thrilling and full of hope as it is good and beautiful, but it is not easy. How could it be? How could the abounding life of the Father, Son, and Spirit come to expression in us without pain? Think about it. How could the freedom or joy or love of Jesus Christ come to us without something of a cutting edge? *We are in the dark.* Our way of being, of living, of life is the fruit of blindness. His presence, good and beautiful as it is, necessarily exposes *our* darkness. Such exposure is painful. For it is neither theoretical nor impersonal. What is exposed by the outright life of Jesus is the mess we have made of ours.

In the dark room of our soul there shines a Christological light, and in this light we glimpse possibilities for ourselves that we never dared dream. We encounter the fact that we have a future, a destiny, a glory. We suddenly know we are not alone, not abandoned or rejected, that we never have been and never will be, that we are included in a communion of overflowing life, that we belong to something beautiful. We see the Father's unflinching heart and His abiding love for us. We are amazed and thrilled and full of hope. But it is precisely in this moment of hope that we begin to hurt. For when the light of Christ shines, not only does it illuminate our stunning destiny; it also exposes the fact that we have lost our minds. In glimpsing home, we know instantly that we are wallowing in the far country of fear. Our salvation in Christ reveals the utter lostness of our own minds.

"Thou art Mine!" is the astonishing and joyous Word of the Father addressing us in Jesus—forever. But such a blessed and liberating Word has an inevitable echo: "Thou fool who lives in darkness." For seeing ourselves embraced by the Father shows us life, and in seeing life, we know we are not living it, that we have fallen short, that we have made a mess of ourselves. Now we see our life not as *life* at all, but as a form of sadness. As Jesus Christ pierces the veil of our blindness, as we discover the beauty and strength of the Father's heart and see ourselves loved and embraced, we become aware of the great and terrible chasm between who we *are* in Christ and who we *believe* we are. Such a discovery baptizes our souls with assurance, but it also stirs up dread.

Don't you see what is happening in our lives? We belong to the Father, Son, and Spirit. We are included in the trinitarian circle of shared life. Jesus meets us where we are in our fallen minds. But the presence of the beloved Son who knows the Father in the fellowship of the Spirit is inherently troubling.

Do you remember the story of Peter fishing with Jesus? After Jesus had finished preaching from the boat, he told Peter to casts his nets out into the deeper water. Peter had fished all night and caught nothing, but he was willing to listen to Jesus. When he cast where Jesus had told him, he caught so many fish that the nets began to break. Peter was thrilled—*and troubled.* In fact, Peter said: "Depart from me Lord, for I am a sinful man" (Luke 5:8).

Jesus does not come to us as an abstract idea that we can think about in our leisure. He does not come to us as an idea at all. He comes as a person—beautiful, free, and alive in the joy of the Father's embrace. He comes as the one anointed in the Spirit. Such beauty, such freedom, such life disturbs us to the core of our being. How could it not? For *he* finds *us* in *our darkness.* He is *the other* in our lives who will not go away, *the other* whose presence quickens us with hope and rocks our illusory world. For in his presence we feel loved and wayward at the same time.

Herein lies the crisis of our existence. Jesus Christ loves us too much to leave us lost and doomed in our mythology. Yet his presence inevitably exposes our living as bound in darkness and death. His sharing his mind with us sets a new world before us, confronting us with a breathtaking vision of his Father and of ourselves and others. This vision searches through our souls, faithfully revealing both that we are loved and cherished and included, *and* that we are a long way from living in the joy of the Father's embrace.

Such exposure hurts like hell. Jesus, of course, intends us no harm. The crucible of his presence is intended to awaken us, to give us solid hope, and to summon us to respond with all of our heart, soul, mind, and strength. His faithfulness to share his knowledge of the Father's heart with us in our darkness means that we now know there is a beautiful life for us to live, *and* that we have not been living it. The pain of such incongruence is a command to stand on our feet, to forsake the darkness, and to believe in the Father's heart. As surely as "Thou fool who lives in darkness" inevitably follows the great and blessed "Thou art Mine!" addressing us in Jesus, so comes the command of the Father's heart, "Rise, My beloved, receive My love and live."

Chapter 11

The Dastardly Trick

There is another, however, who drafts behind the shafts of Jesus' light, exploiting its authority and the pain of its exposure. This "other" turns the command of the Father's heart from astonished and joyous freedom into fearful condemnation. Like a crouching lion, he waits until the love of the Father inevitably stings, until in hearing "Thou art Mine," we also hear "Thou fool who lives in darkness." In the moment between "Thou fool who lives in darkness" and "Rise, My beloved, receive My love and live," the lion pounces for the kill. He takes "Thou fool" and twists it into "I am not." *I am not acceptable. I am not loved, not included, not special. I am not good enough, not going to make it, not worthy. I am not important. See, fools are not loved by God. God is the watcher and His own word to you is that you are a failure. You are doomed. Do you not hear: "Thou fool who lives in darkness?"*

Having no power of his own, the evil one uses the power of Jesus' penetrating revelation to preach his own dastardly sermon, weaving a spell of ontological condemnation out of the truth's exposure of our darkness. The pump is primed and we don't even know it. Like John and Stephanie, we have eyes to see "I am not acceptable" everywhere we look. And life, our parents, our husbands or wives, our friends, and circumstances and events provide ample evidence to confirm the lie.

In his passionate love Jesus has slipped through the smoke screens and found you in your own fallen mind. The presence in your darkness of the Son who knows his Father is a recipe both for liberation and for serious pain—and not one without the other. The Son intends your pain to convince you that there is a very real problem, thereby engaging you in personal deliverance. But there is one who exploits Jesus' good will and his inescapable presence. The evil one takes your pain, the redemptive pain that cuts you to the quick when Jesus shares his Father's love with you, and he uses that pain to whisper condemnation. He turns family embarrassment into shame. He confirms the mythological deity out of the hurt caused by Jesus' knowledge of the Father's heart.

Stop and take this in. Evil confirms our false god out of the hurt caused by the *Father's love*. He takes the proper and exposing impact of Jesus' outright assurance and peace, and twists it into a lie—and he tangles the name of Jesus Christ into the lie itself. Jesus calls him "the father of lies" for good reason. He is a liar, and his lies convince you that your pain, your anxious imagination, is the truth of god.

Let me give you a picture of how this works. Many years ago, my wife and I got into a debate about the color of our apartment walls. I contended that they were obviously white. She argued that they were off-white. So, to prove my point, I grabbed a piece of typing paper and held it next to the wall. Instantly I knew I was wrong. The whiteness of the typing paper revealed the walls to be anything but white.

This is what happens to us as Jesus penetrates our fallen minds. His whiteness exposes our lives as anything but white. His knowledge of the Father's heart, his unearthly assurance and peace, his joy and abounding freedom reveal that we are living like a church mouse in fear and hiding. Such exposure creates pain in us. To be sure, Jesus' hope gives us hope, his peace and assurance give us peace and assurance, but they also burn. For his own peace puts its finger on our dis-ease and makes us feel it. His rest proves we are running. His life exposes our self-generated religion as death. His freedom with his Father is a mirror in which we see ourselves not free in the love of the Father at all, but trembling and sad and broken.

Do you see what is happening? Jesus' unearthly assurance touches our profound insecurity. It is the whiteness of his Father's forgiveness itself that makes us feel the darkness of our guilt. The incongruence is intended to send us running to the Father's arms for our healing. If we knew the Father's heart, if we believed in His lavish forgiveness, then the exposure of our darkness would function as a command, freeing us to stand and bring our guilt and fear and insecurity to be bathed in the Father's love. But the accuser is waiting for such a moment. He takes our insecurity and guilt and fear and twists them into a false god. As the Father's face is tarred with our guilt, as His eyes are painted with our fear, the watching, eager judge is born in the corners of our soul.

As Jesus shares the Father's love with us, we begin to see where and when and how we have failed to receive His love. We know we are wayward sons and daughters. But before we can receive His endless love into our brokenness, the accuser whispers, *Wayward is right. Just look at you!* In a split second, the exposing and liberating love of the Father is twisted into, *I am not loveable, I am not acceptable and never will be.* Realizing our waywardness is fodder for the accuser's deceit.

It is a dastardly trick. Do you see it? First there is the Father's love and forgiveness, flowing out of the way He loves His Son. Jesus shares this love and forgiveness with us so that we can experience their freedom in the Spirit. As he does, we feel our guilt. In knowing this love, we know we have not lived in its joy. And here, in the exposing light of the love and forgiveness of the Father, the liar takes our guilt and uses it to create in *our minds* a false god who is incapable of forgiveness. He waits until the Father's forgiveness reveals our guilt and then takes our guilt and turns it into an unforgiving deity in our heads. We are left with a guilty conscience before an unforgiving god, with nowhere to go.

Chapter 12

Running

We are so inept; we don't know what is happening. Capitalizing on the outright strength of the Father's exposing forgiveness, evil whispers "I am not" in our ears and it seems the most obvious thing in the world. *Of course. I am not worthy, not loveable, not acceptable. The proof is everywhere. How could god even look at me?* Ashamed and hopeless, outgunned and trapped, we know we are doomed. We dare not face what this means—rejection, abandonment, the abyss. The pain of it all is intolerable. So we run. With all our might, we run. Why shouldn't we? What option do we really have? Off we go on a 30-year bender. We call it love. We call it marriage and friendship. We call it work and vision, and even a burden for the lost and the helpless. We may even call it worship and obedience to the Lord. But it is our pain and our false god driving us to hide, driving us to find something somewhere that gives us a moment's relief.

In the darkness of the twisting lie, we actually run from our Savior and hide from the Father's delight. Confused, scared, and hopeless, we run from the Father's forgiveness into false religion to appease our mythological deity. If we would only stop and think! The Father loves us—always has and always will. He forgives. We are embraced forever. If we would only cry out for help! But how could we possibly stop? How could we possibly face this god of ours? Who wants to run into the arms of an unforgiving Ogre with "I am not acceptable" ringing in his ears? Who wants to be still long enough to hear the voice of this dreadful god and face the hell of its judgment?

So we set sail on a journey to save ourselves from our pain. John chose work, then medication, then leaning on his wife to mend his aching soul, all the while dying inside and leaving a trail of relational wreckage behind him. Stephanie chose the imaginary perfection of niceness and denial. How could she possibly look at herself? That would mean feeling the pain of "I am not acceptable" in the face of her mythological, unforgiving god, and thus standing eye to eye with the threat of utter abandonment. Who can face such a nightmare? So she ran by being nice and pretending that all was well. All hands on her emotional deck were summoned to support her in her game of pretending, which left her emotionally unavailable for her husband and family. Do you remember Saul and Ehud? They ran by embracing their mythology and by creating a religion within it that allowed them to feel good about themselves. And that feeling was so precious to them that they lived on red alert, ready to draw their guns and shoot down anything that hinted at a threat to their religious system—even the Father's Son incarnate.

We run too. What real choice do we have? Don't you see? We spend so much of our lives running, hiding, working to deal with our fear. The pain is intolerable. So we pretend it is not there. We numb it with entertainment or busyness or some form of narcotic. We lean on others to make us feel better. We dream a dream that will prove we are worthy, and we protect it with a vengeance, even when it doesn't work.

Jesus does not come to us with a great theological treatise under his arm. He does not come with a brain drill and a funnel to pour accurate information into our heads. He simply and masterfully enters into our darkness, and his presence inevitably creates pain. His knowledge of the Father's love points out where and when and how we are not receiving His love. Evil exploits the exposure, whispers, "I am not acceptable," and proves the mythological deity in our heads. We are left holding the bag of our unacceptability while standing before an unforgiving god. As though someone has touched the rawest nerve in our being, we recoil, launching ourselves for a 30 or 40, or maybe even an 80-year run.

Stop and think about it. Why are you so driven to work? What are you trying to prove, and to whom? Don't get me wrong. Work is good, and we should be passionate about it. For we are made to participate in the creative blessing of the Father, Son, and Spirit. But when work is driven by "I am not acceptable" and by our mythological deity who watches us like a hawk, or by lust for money to buy more toys to entertain us in our pain, the joy of work is utterly silenced. There is all the difference in the world between working out of the Father's embrace and doing the exact same work out of insecurity and fear and pain. The one is the free expression of the Father's love reaching out in the service of His children, the other is a self-salvation scheme, a long attempt to justify ourselves, a form of entertainment, or a drug, each doomed to fail us and leave us more afflicted than ever—not to mention what they do to our relationships in the process.

We are dying inside, so like a tick on a hound[7] we attach ourselves to others, hoping to get the life from them that we do not have in ourselves. Like John, we walk into the room of our relationships with an invisible sign blaring, *"Fix me. Fix me. Fix me."* Think about it. Think of the subtle yet terrible pressure we put on those around us to make us feel good. Think of how much time we spend manipulating people. Don't you see how skilled we are at shaming and seducing, how we use our moods, our sighs, our anger and false promises to shuffle the world, so that our own wounds might be salved and we might feel good about ourselves? Have you ever thought about what happens when you leave the room?[8]

What hurt we have caused in our absence. "Elvis has left the building." We have checked out. The fear has shut us down. Years ago we flipped onto cruise control, busying ourselves with every important thing. We all know the script, but what is a script with a closed soul? As my friend Billy Blue says, "She looks like an angel, but she's a cripple on the inside." We cannot give what we do not have, so we work to look the part and hope no one knows the difference. Hiding behind the script, we rob our husbands and wives and friends of real fellowship and shared life. Do you not see how your absence has left your spouse without a friend? You are not there. Your wife has no real partner to share life with her, no soul-mate to share her tears. You don't even know she is crying. "Pass the mashed potatoes. Did you see the Braves play last night?"

What if our noble causes turn out to be mostly entertainment for our own latent sorrow? What if our wonderful passion to help turns out to be a narcotic? We stay busy for others, but could it be that our busyness is actually for us? Could our sacrifice be another way of saving ourselves from our sorrow, a pat of affirmation on our own backs? Don't you see how much emotional energy we use protecting ourselves, hiding, keeping our façade stable, managing our inner world, trying to keep the wheels from coming off? The pain is real, and it is intolerable. Life becomes a long, self-centered quest to find relief.

The presence of the Father's Son in our darkness means it does not have to be this way. He brings a beautiful life for us to live.

---

[7] I am indebted to Gary Arinder for this analogy.

[8] See the story of Mrs. Fidget in my book *The Great Dance* (Jackson: Perichoresis Press, 2000; Vancouver: Regent College Publishing, 2005), 69ff., 78ff.

Chapter 13

The Good Shepherd

The dilemma for Jesus is that he is determined we know his Father's heart and live in its freedom, yet he will not cross the boundaries of our personhood and make our decisions for us. He will not wave a magic wand and undo our wrong-headedness. Jesus is not a co-dependent savior. He does not need to be needed. He will not reach into our souls and take away the pain. But why not? That would be a quick and easy way around the problem. Just speak the "Word" and erase the hard drive of our fallen minds. Then reconfigure our default settings so that we could see the truth, receive it, and live in its joy. As simple and easy as this may sound, it cannot work this way.

To begin with, the life of the Father, Son, and Spirit is not mechanical. At its heart, the trinitarian life involves three distinct persons, three distinct wills, giving themselves completely in love and fellowship to one another, yet without enmeshment. So how could we possibly participate in this kind of life in a robotic way that bypasses our own wills? Love involves the decision of the heart, mind, and will. If we are to experience this life, we must possess our own hearts, minds and wills and we must choose to participate in it. To wave the magic wand would be to utterly annihilate us as persons.

If Jesus crossed into our minds and made our decisions for us, if he waved the wand, there would be no *us* left to taste and feel and experience the trinitarian life. What is a person without a heart, a mind, and a will? We would be left no more than religious robots, and the staggering dream of the Father for *us* would die. While such a thought is as unthinkable for the Father, Son, and Spirit as abandoning us in our mythology, it creates a serious dilemma.

As the Father will never become the Son or the Spirit, and the Son and Spirit will never become one another or the Father, yet the Father, Son, and Spirit are one in self-giving love and mutual knowing, so this God grants, treasures, and guards the reality of our distinctness. For our distinctness is the only path to *our* sharing in the trinitarian life. Yet in our sacred distinctness, we are trapped in the delusion of our fallen minds. The *we* who must choose to participate in the trinitarian life are blind as bats, locked into a dreadful cycle of wrong belief and anxiety, projection and misperception. We see only the brooding, disapproving god of our anxious imaginations. We live out the trinitarian life, so freely shared with us, through our fear-twisted vision and its terrifying insecurity. With our souls baptized in anxiety, lost in the whisper "I am not acceptable," we run. We have done so our whole lives, habitually so.

Jesus wants *persons*, not religious machines. He wants *us* discerning life from death, good from evil, light from darkness, embracing his light with all our heart, soul, mind, and strength. He wants *us* alive with his knowledge of his Father's heart, filled and overflowing with his peace and unearthly assurance, free from our imprisoning darkness, free to care, free to forgive, free to love, free to know and be known. He wants us free to give ourselves for others, and free to receive their self-giving in fellowship. His passion is that we experience, in our relationships with one another and with the whole creation, the life he has with his Father in the Spirit.

But we are so broken. How can we trust that Jesus' knowledge of the Father's heart is anything more than another trick of the gods, setting us up for greater disappointment? Are we not like an abused dog staring across the yard at food?[9] How can we possibly muster the courage to walk across the yard of our abuse, to venture from our "I am not" and our "god" into the new world of Jesus' Father and His "Thou art Mine?" We may be miserable, sad, and lonely; we may be hiding and broken, and our misery may be intensified to the boiling point by the knowledge of the Father's heart, but our fallen minds fit like old shoes. Our mythology is the safest place we know. How can we embrace these rumors of being loved? How can we dare trust this peace? *Forgiveness? How could such a thing be possible for me?* How can we believe, "Rise, My beloved, receive My love and live," when our god is so eager to reject, watching every move we make with his disapproving heart? This is the crisis of our existence. We must live with the presence of Jesus Christ.

---

[9] The imagery of an abused puppy struggling to accept new-found acceptance comes from Dr. Bruce Wauchope's lecture, "The Gospel and Mental Health." This lecture is available at <www.perichoresis.org>.

Like a house cat standing before an open door, we face an unknown world in Christ. It is full of promise, yet it is *unknown,* its goodness inconceivable. It may be an illusion. *Better to stay just inside the door and watch. Better the devil we know than the devil we don't. Perhaps I won't have to be real before Jesus and take responsibility for myself. Perhaps I can pretend everything is just fine. Perhaps Jesus will sweep me up and take it all away.* But Jesus offers no "Calgon" moment. He will not sweep us up and take away our pain. But neither will he forsake us in our mythology.

Is Jesus an ivory-tower academic out of touch with our human trauma? Does he not know what it means to us to hear him speak? Is he unaware of how scary it is to face him, and to face him while hearing the whisper? Is he oblivious to the outright pain of our acknowledging that there is more, that we belong to something vast and deep and beautiful, when all we have ever known is "I am not acceptable" and our mythological deity? Does Jesus not know the crucible?

Of course he does. Isn't this why Jesus is so patient with us, why he does not come crashing into our lives like a charging elephant? Isn't this why he lets us cruise for a while on autopilot? He surely hates our denial, for he knows the beautiful life he shares with us, yet in his love he honors where we are in our own mythological worlds. Jesus addresses us in full knowledge of where we actually are in our confusion, even our religious confusion. He knows what we feel today in our skewed vision. He knows what we do and do not see. He knows how deeply we have embraced the whisper, "I am not important," and he knows how seriously we believe in our god. He accepts us as we are. He gives us space and time and freedom to do what we want, to reach out for any fruit in the universe, to live out our theories and our self-salvation schemes, to pretend, to medicate, to find another savior.

The love of Jesus is as endless as his goodness. It is as constant as it is true. And his love throws us into profound crisis. The impossible union between the beloved Son who knows his Father and fear-stricken Adam, trembling and hiding in the bushes, is now within *us.* "Rise, My beloved" and "I am not acceptable" swirl within our own souls. The one is too good to be true, the other is unbearable. We live in the crucible of response. The Good Shepherd is faithful to accept us and walk with us. He is faithful to share himself with us, and to create the crisis of our liberation, all the while running the risk of our choosing the lie and its god and hating him forever.

Chapter 14

The Decision

We belong to the triune God—we always have and we always will. We are alive with the trinitarian life, yet in the distinctness of our own minds, hearts, and wills, we do not get it, and we unwittingly poison this life by imposing our mythology upon it. But Jesus Christ is ever faithful to address us, faithful to find a reconciling foothold in our fallen minds, faithful to share himself with us. He is the true and faithful witness. He will not cross the boundaries of our personhood, but he does cross the great and terrible chasm of our fallenness.

Without Jesus Christ's faithfulness to share himself with us, without his prophetic skill penetrating our alien vision in the Spirit's genius, we would have no choice but to embrace our darkness and live in its miserable doom. All of our philosophical talk of free will would be utter nonsense. Left to ourselves, we would be free only to choose what our fallen minds perceive. We would be trapped in our darkness, forced to live out the trinitarian life, so freely shared with us, through our own anxiety and wrong-headedness, projection and misperception. But we do have a choice. Given that Jesus Christ knows the Father, given that he dwells in our darkness, and given that he is sharing his knowledge of the Father's heart with us all, a new world stands before us.

Indeed, the faithfulness of Jesus Christ means not only that we have a choice, but also that we have no choice but to exercise it. We *must* choose. Jesus Christ's sharing his mind with us means we must decide what we will believe. Which world will we choose to live in, our own or his? Guarding our personal distinctness, yet ever faithful to the reality of our inclusion, Jesus' presence forces the issue—my light or your darkness, my way of seeing or yours, my heaven or your hell?

It is here in this crucible of Jesus' presence, of real hope and longing and hurt, that the command of our salvation works within us. As Jesus' knowledge of the Father's heart pierces our wrong-headedness, we stand before a fork in the road. What will we believe? What will we believe about God? *Is this news of the Father and His endless love real, or is the god that seems so obvious to me the true God? Who am I? There are two versions of me, the one I see in the light of Christ, and the other I have always known. Which is the real me? Do I stand on the edge of the abyss? Am I forsaken? Is life a dream? Or do I exist in relationship with the triune God and therefore stand commanded and free to embrace this truth and live in its joy?*

The presence of Jesus Christ inside our fallen minds is a constant command, summoning us out of our denial, calling us to give up our self-generated religions and our false saviors, to step out of our tragic nightmare and receive the love of the Father. What will you do with Jesus' knowledge of the Father's heart? To ignore it is to embrace a world you now know is empty and sad and broken. To go forward, you must take responsibility for yourself and what you believe, you must stare your demons in the face and learn to believe the truth in your pain.

Chapter 15

Facing Pain[10]

There is no other way. We must venture forth; we must embrace the crisis and trust Jesus for ourselves. The old self, the self in bondage, must be undone. And Jesus will not wave the magic wand. We must face our darkness and step through its fear into the new world of Jesus Christ. He will not push us, but neither will he go away. In the knowledge of the Father's lavish love, Jesus confronts us in our fearful mythology. Even as we run from him and his pain-inducing light, he finds us. The stormy seas of our delusion offer no place to hide from our brother. He searches us out. He speaks. We stand before him, responsible for ourselves and what we now believe, summoned to sanity and life. Which world will we live in?

Jesus crosses the chasms of our wrong-headedness. He pierces the veil of our blindness. He shares his knowledge of the Father's heart with us. He knows our trauma. He knows the abuse we have suffered. He knows the anguish we have endured, the grief, the heartache, the woe and sorrow of our lives. He is well aware of our family system and its dysfunction, of what it groomed us to be from our mother's womb. He sees our father's rejection and how it shut us down and how the evil one exploits it. He sees our mother's absence and the family habits of darkness of which we are an unwitting, yet willing part. He sees how we were made to feel responsible for others. He knows our shame. He knows where we are in our fallen minds.

Jesus has made his way into our mythological world with his knowledge of the Father's love. He is full of compassion, and inescapable. Like it or not, his presence means that we are summoned to take

---

[10] My discussion of facing pain grows out of years of conversation with Steve Horn, my Thursday morning pastor's group, friends in recovery, Dr. Bruce Wauchope, and not least out of my own life and struggles.

responsibility for what we believe, for what we feel, for what we think and do. No more blame. For he has penetrated our trauma, our wounds, our brokenness with his light. There is no place in the universe of the fallen mind, or in the terror of the human wound, that Jesus Christ has not traversed and found his Father's heart within. And there is no place where he fails to share with us what he knows in the Father's arms.

"All I want to know right now is what you believe in. And what it means for you to be alive. Will you stand here in this fire with me? Are you ready for another life?"[11] These words echo the question of our faithful brother, the seasoned prophet, the true and faithful witness, addressing us in his infinite tenderness: "What do you seek?" (John 1:38)

> Do you want life? Are you prepared to see your darkness? I will share the truth with you, but you must stand and walk with me. I will show you how to undo your darkness, but you must face it. I bring my Father's healing love to wash the feet of your wounds, but you must let me.

We are eternally loved and accepted by the Father Himself. We are addressed by His Son in the power of the Spirit. We stand commanded: "Rise, My beloved, receive My love and live." But to receive the love of the Father, to know it, to experience its joy, we must face what is keeping us from believing. We must repent and believe, our fallen minds must be undone and restructured in truth. There is no other way. It is no use wanting heaven without facing our hell, or craving a cure without acknowledging our pain. The road to healing, to heaven, to experiencing the Father's love, runs straight into the belly of the beast. We must face the lie and the liar, and the terrible god of our anxious imaginations. We must face what we have done to ourselves and to others in our darkness. We must acknowledge our pain and own up to our denial, our addictions, our absence and our endless attempts to save ourselves. The Father's Son, our brother, meets us here, in the trenches of our brokenness. His joy awaits us in our fear. Our god has no teeth.

Read carefully this beautiful poem by Dr. Bruce Wauchope:

---

[11] From the song, "Everything Is Different Now," by Don Henley, Scott F. Crago and Timothy Drury, from the CD, *Don Henley: Inside Job* (Warner Brothers, Records Inc., 2000).

Pearl

Emergent pain has overtaken my consciousness.
Searing, derailing
A river, murky
its fear has carried me away
I've lost my footing
There is no bottom

Out of my depth I yell,
"Share what he knows, for I don't
Give me what I can't feel
he knows your face, he knows your hugs, he knows"

Sitting still in the river, I face and peer into the depths.
Down I sit, down I go
An indistinct abyss yawns at me
totally black and bottomless

Then eventually it appears
Lucent and white
Torn substance gives way
The frayed black edges cannot hold it back
Emergent life
A pearl

It is him in me and me in him
Christ in me and me in Christ
A pearl
The door to the paved streets, us of great price

Bottomless abyss my foot
it has a base
it has torn and life is emerging
I will not go back

—Bruce Wauchope, 2006

Questions for Reflection

(1) Why does the Father's love hurt?

(2) Do you think Jesus could share himself with you without exposing your own darkness?

(3) Reflect on this statement: "Jesus does not come to us with a great theological treatise under his arm. He does not come with a brain drill and a funnel to pour accurate information into our heads. He simply and masterfully enters into our darkness, and his presence inevitably creates pain."

(4) List the ways in which you run from the pain of Jesus' presence.

(5) What does your spiritual pain feel like? What do you do to avoid it? What does your avoidance say to those you love?

(6) What is your primary "I am not?" How did you come to believe it? Can you remember the first time it crossed your mind?

(7) Why doesn't Jesus just wave the magic wand and make your life perfect?

(8) Is there a difference between the way you want others to see you and the way they actually do see you?

(9) Where do you feel most at home? Why?

(10) In what ways, places or situations do the words, "Rise, My beloved, receive My love and live" and "I am not acceptable" battle within you?

(11) What will you regret in heaven when you discover that the Father has always loved you as he loves Jesus?

Part 4

Come Unto Me

Chapter 16

You Belong to the Father

Following on the heels of Jesus' exclusive declaration, "No one knows the Father, but the Son," comes his famous command:

> Come unto Me, all who are weary and heavy-laden, and I will give you rest. Take My yoke upon you, and learn from Me, for I am gentle and humble in heart; and you shall find rest for your souls. For My yoke is easy, and My load is light (Matthew 11:28–30).

These are the words of the Father's Son, our brother, speaking to us inside our fallen minds. Do not allow the evil one to twist Jesus' "Come unto Me" into another proof of "I am not." Of course, "Come unto Me" means you are lost. Why would Jesus command you to come to him if you were already with him? But the truth is, you *are* with him. You are separated from Jesus Christ and his Father only in your own mind—separated only by your own wrong-headed believing, lost only in your own darkness.[12] You are not lost to Jesus. He has found you in your mythological world, and he summons you to step out of it into the freedom and joy of his light.

Jesus is commanding you to reject the darkness and to receive his light. His command is the command of belonging to his Father: "Thou art Mine! Now rise, forsake the darkness, receive My knowledge of the Father, and live." The strategy of evil is to attack your vision of the Father's heart. The devil is not a gentleman, as my friend David Upshaw says. He has no intention of playing fair. His aim is to destroy any

---

[12] For more on our identity in Christ and being lost in our own minds, see C. Baxter Kruger, *The Secret*. This book is available as a free download from <www.perichoresis.org.>

notion you have of the Father, and in so doing to leave you hiding from the unaccepting god of your imagination. Having no real authority in himself, the evil one misuses the light of Jesus.

Of course the light of Christ exposes your darkness. Seeing yourself in the arms of the Father's love gives you hope and also reveals that you are living as a homeless and pitiful beggar. This is what I have called "family embarrassment." The exposure is real and it hurts, but it is exposure *within* the family. You belong to the Father, Son, and Spirit. You are included in the trinitarian family forever. The trick of evil is to take the exposure of your blindness and your family disloyalty and craft them into proof that you do not belong to the family *at all*—you are separated from God.

Do not confuse your identity with your experience. You can be a member of the family and not live in its truth or joy. But that never means that you are therefore excluded from the family—cut off, rejected. The Father is not that fickle. He was Father before creation. His relationship with you flows out of His relationship with His Son and Spirit. Stop and think. Do you see ambiguity on the Father's face as He looks at His Son? Do you see eagerness to judge? Do you see a disapproving heart? Do you see indifference or disinterest in the Father's eyes? The way the Father loves His Son is the way He loves you. There are not two Fathers, the Father of Jesus and then a different Father with a different heart who relates to you. Jesus' Father loves. He does not change. His love is strong. His love is pure.

Evil takes Jesus' exposure of your waywardness and turns it into a statement about the Father Himself. But think about it. Can you change the Father? Can you actually alter the way the Father relates to His Son? Are you so powerful as to be able to tamper with the being of the triune God?

Note this carefully: What you do or do not do, what you believe or do not believe, has no power at all to alter the Father's love or your place in the trinitarian family. There is no person, power, or event in the universe that can change the Father or your belonging to Him in Jesus. Your blindness, your fallen mind, and your mythology do not affect the Father's arms, and never will, but they do affect the way *you see and relate to Him*. The presence of the Father's Son—in the beauty and joy and freedom of their relationship in the fellowship of the Spirit—inevitably exposes that you are not being true to yourself as the Father's beloved. Evil takes the exposure and proceeds with theological abuse in your head. He turns the revelation of your waywardness into a statement about *God* and about your *identity*. "Wayward" becomes *I am not worthy. Therefore God could not like me. I am unacceptable. I do not belong, and never will.* But think about it. Even the word "wayward" is a family word. Could you be wayward if you do not belong? Could you be lost if you have no home?

Go back to the truth of the Father's heart and to your identity as His beloved child. You have always belonged to the Father, Son, and Spirit, and always will. Jesus has come to find you in your mythology, where you cannot believe the Father's heart, where you are lost in the lie and its darkness and cannot see the Father's face. "Come unto Me" means that Jesus Christ has crossed all worlds to find you. He has braved the seas of your illusions to find your heart. He is standing inside your darkness when he commands you to come to him. Dare to trust him.

The strange thing is that your pain is the proof that you belong to the triune God, proof that Jesus Christ is faithful to you, proof that *he* has found *you* in your *darkness*. Don't you see? It is because you are part of the family, part of the abounding life of the Father, Son, and Spirit that the exposure of your waywardness hurts so profoundly. If you had no home, hearing of it would not make you homesick. If you did not belong to the triune God, you would have no notion of glory, so the rumors of the far-off land, and of the Father's gaze would not speak so deeply to your heart. If you were never meant to see His face, missing it wouldn't trouble you at all.

But you are part of the trinitarian family. You do belong to glory. You are included in the abounding life of the Father, Son and Spirit, and you are meant to see His face and live in the freedom of His lavish embrace. Thus the exposure of your waywardness cuts you to the quick. The pain is proof that you belong, proof that your faithful brother has found you, and found you in your darkness. And it is proof that you can receive the Father's love.

The presence of Jesus awakens you in your darkness and confusion. You know you are real. You feel yourself and your sorrow. You run. You have done so all your life, in one form or another. You are part of a family system that has serious expertise in running, in hiding, in pretending, in searching for another savior and another salvation. It stretches back for generations. You are part of the system. You were trained from birth to participate in the family pattern. You were assigned a role in the family self-salvation scheme and you have lost your true self in living it out.

Are you exhausted from running? Have the wheels come off? Are you worn out from trying to hold it all together, from trying to keep things under control, from the incessant effort to manage your inner world? Are you tired of dying and feeling dead? Are you tired of pretending? Your sadness, your misery, the sheer uncomfortableness of your being, are telling you that you belong to the Father, Son, and Spirit, *and* that there is a problem. The pain is telling you that the Father's Son has found you, *and* that you are not living in the Father's embrace, *and* that your life can be different.

"Come unto Me" means there is a new life for you to live. In the freedom of Jesus' heart, in the presence of his sanity and faith and courage, you have freedom to say "no" to what you believe about your god. In Jesus' unearthly assurance you can take responsibility for yourself and for what you have done in your pain. In his acceptance, you can stop blaming your parents, your husband, your wife. You can stop blaming everyone else in the world but yourself for your sadness, your anger, your fear, your hard life. In Jesus' knowledge that you belong to the Father, you can face the fact that you have believed the lie. Yes, the lie was confirmed a thousand times by others, by your father and mother, by your brothers and sisters, by your husband or wife, by events and traumas, by the cards you were dealt—even by the Church. Yes, the "proof" is everywhere. But Jesus Christ has penetrated everyone's fault, and the lie itself, and found you in your deepest darkness. His presence commands you to come to him—to believe, to receive the Father's love and live.

He gives you his rest: As you feel his rest, you can face what is keeping you from resting in it. If Jesus is sharing his own peace with you—and he is, and will never withdraw it—then what is keeping you from experiencing his peace? Why the turmoil? Why are you so frantic? Why the running? Is it because you do not belong to the Father, Son, and Spirit? Is it because Jesus is playing some kind of game with you, where he gives you his peace and then takes it away? Of course not. You belong to the Father, Son and Spirit. Jesus is steadfast in his sharing himself with you. The problem is not with the triune God. The problem is in your own mind.

Clinging to our own way of seeing God is saying to Jesus that he is dead wrong about his. As my firend Ken Blue says, the question is: Can Jesus be trusted? Are we willing to be taught by Jesus, or are we demanding that he repent? Sin is our insistence that Jesus repent, that give up his vision of his Father and join us in our notion of god. "Come unto Me" means that we do not have to live in our own worlds. We can participate in Jesus'. He bids us to take sides with him against our false god and his debilitating verdict.

Chapter 17

Finding Rest

To find rest for your soul, look with Jesus into his Father's eyes. Accept yourself as the Father's beloved child. Acknowledge that the Father Himself is proud of you. In the freedom of His pride, acknowledge that you are blind. Face the fact that something within you is hesitant to believe. Confess that something within your own heart whispers, "No, it cannot be this simple. God cannot be this good. I could not be this wrong." As the beautiful life of Jesus with his Father and Spirit exposes your hiding and pretending, your shallowness and fear, do not run. Do not shut down. Do not pretend. Stop and face the pain. Embrace the exposure, own it, take responsibility for it, and right there in the midst of the pain dare to look into the Father's face. It is all about receiving the Father's love. "Come unto Me" means nothing more than, "Receive my knowledge of my Father and believe in my Father's love. Declare war on your own vision of god and his neglect, his indifference, his eagerness to judge. Listen to me, your brother. I know the Father's heart."

Inside your mind and heart there are two different visions of God: the god you have created in the darkness, and the Father, Son, and Spirit. Which God do you believe in now, at this moment? Who is your God today? Stop and take a moment to think about your failures. Think of what you have done wrong, and all the of things that make you feel ashamed. Think of the whisper. Think of what you hope no one ever knows about you. Now, look at all of these things and see the Father's compassion. Do you honestly think that Jesus' Father is unaware of your secret list of personal disasters? Is He blind to your striving and hiding and pretending? Does He not see the religions we have created in our darkness? Do you believe that He has turned away from you, that He cannot bear to look upon such a mess? Jesus' Father loves. He sees the mess and His heart never flinches. He loves *you.*

The irony of the kingdom of the Father, Son, and Spirit is that it is in facing ourselves, in being honest about what we have done and not done, in staring our shame in the face and feeling the sheer sadness of it all, that we encounter the Father's unflinching heart. How can this be? All these years you have believed you are not worthy, not good enough, too bad for His love. Now you hear that it is in being honest with your failures that you get new eyes to see His face. Evil twists forgiveness into an unforgiving god, but Jesus meets you in that fear with his Father's love. "It is not *those* who are healthy who need a doctor, but those who are sick: I did not come to call the righteous, but sinners" (Mark 2:17).

> Father, in the freedom of your endless love and in the safety of your embrace, I acknowledge to you that something happens to me and I get lost in the darkness. Instead of living in your joy, I get crippled inside. I change. Instead of receiving your love, my soul is disturbed. I become needy. I shut down and withdraw. I become self-centered, angry and frustrated. In my pain I hurt those I love. I waste time and life. I am embarrassed. I am scared to look at myself. Forgive me for blaming others for my problems. Speak to my soul, Father. Tell me again that there is more to me than I know. Help me believe that my existence, my life, my future is part of yours. Help me see that facing my life and my hurt means liberation and fullness, not death. Jesus, give me your eyes. Help me to see myself as you do. Holy Spirit, bear witness to my soul that I belong to Jesus and his Father forever. Show me where and when and how I am not receiving Jesus' Father's love. Show me how my fear is attached to people and places, events and smells and things. Transform the triggers and associations of evil into sacraments of the Father's love. Forgive me for what I have done and said, and for what I have not done and not said to your children.

Chapter 18

Henry

I have an old missionary friend; let's call him Henry. I always thought the world of Henry; he seemed to be so real, so dedicated, so passionate. But a few years ago, Henry popped back into my life. He looked like death eating a cracker. Henry had given up, given up on himself, on his mission, on God, on everything. He'd lost his wife. He didn't even know where his kids were. He was so torn up, he couldn't even cry about it. For a long time he just sat there dry as a bone. He didn't even look human. All the parts were there, but his face and eyes and skin looked as if he had swallowed a vacuum cleaner.

Henry had worked his fingers to the bone for 18 years, 3 months and 14 days, passionately seeking the glory of God and the salvation of others. Those years were a slow burn, as my friend Steve Horn would say. Spiritual pain crept up the tree of his soul like invisible kudzu, until the light and life were choked out. Today, Henry has a new God and a new salvation to proclaim. But between now and then, there was a stretch of gut-wrenching hell for Henry.

Henry's great breakthrough came when he realized that those 18 years, 3 months, and 14 days were neither for God nor for others. Those years were for Henry. Those were the running years, the hiding and pretending years, the years driven to justify himself, to prove to himself and to his god that his existence was a worthy divine investment.

Henry knows that if the Lord can speak through Balaam's donkey, then he can also use us in our imperfections. But he also knows that we can spend a lot of time serving God and others *for ourselves.* That does not mean that everything we have done is therefore wrong or of no value. It is more like poisoning. Our *self-service* service taints what we are doing. And it certainly keeps us from enjoying our lives and relationships, and not least the Father Himself.

The beautiful thing about Henry's story is the connection between his shame and feeling the Father's love. It was as he tasted the withering embarrassment of his blindness, as he wept over his self-centeredness and its poison, and as he faced his home-grown religion that he felt the Father's acceptance, even approval and delight. I told Henry that there are only two kinds of people in the world: those who are full of crap and know it, and those who are full of crap and don't know it. Facing your crap and feeling the embarrassment of it all is when you hear the Father's voice most clearly. How ironic! You feel the Father's embrace as you confess your mess. For it is only then that you know that He likes *you*.

Think about it. If you have sealed off part of yourself because it is unacceptable, then that part of you never gets to experience the Father's heart. You are hiding yourself from Him and His love. The truth is that the sealed-off, hidden part of you drives the rest of you and your life. It poisons everything else you are doing. The more you run from your brokenness, the more the rest of you is driven to prove that you are whole. Life becomes a long self-centered attempt to justify yourself, hide, or pretend that all is well. You are in it for yourself.

Brokenness gives you new eyes to see the Father's face, and new ears to hear Him say, "Rise, My beloved, receive My love and live." He's been shouting it from the dawn of creation. But who could hear Him? As long as we think we can carve out our own way, who is listening to grace? It is the failures, the broken, the ones who have crashed and burned, the ones who know they cannot make it who get to see the Father. They are the ones who are thrilled at the command, "Come unto Me." For in Jesus' voice they do not hear religion or "I am not." They hear hope. They find liberation. They meet new freedom from themselves and from their own false vision of god.

"Come unto Me" means you can live in the unearthly assurance of the Father's acceptance. No hiding. No pretending. No self-justification. Just the simple belief that Jesus' Father accepts you. That is Henry today—a man who knows the joy of the Father's lavish love. Henry doesn't have to prove anything to himself or to God or to anyone else on the planet. He is not driven to save himself by saving others for God. He doesn't have to be nice or hide or pretend or manipulate. He is free to enjoy his Father with Jesus. And that freedom means that Henry is a real person: honest, present, other-centered. Such is the kingdom of the Father, Son, and Spirit.

> Yes, Lord Jesus, Father's true Son, my faithful savior, I am burdened and heavy-laden. I am tired. I come to you for rest. Open my eyes that I might see. Pull the thread of my wrong-

headedness. Pull it until the whole family rug is undone. Pull it until my guilt unravels into the Father's forgiveness. Pull it until my god vanishes and there is only the Father's face. Teach me to see through the lie. Set me free to embrace your knowledge of the Father's heart. Jump with me into my abyss and show me our Father's arms.

The faithful and true Son of the Father, the one who has seen what we see and felt what we feel, the one who found his Father's heart within the travail of our brokenness, this one says to the world:

Bring your religion to the fire of the Father's embrace. Put the ledger down. Throw your paintbrushes away and learn from me, for I know the Father, and I am gentle and humble in heart. I bring my Father's love into your despair. Do not run, for I will never abandon you. I will be faithful to you until you know as I know, until the freedom of my Father's love fills your heart, and our love overflows into your relationships with one another and with all creation, and my knowledge of my Father covers the earth as the waters cover the sea. Rise, My beloved, receive My love and live.

Questions for Reflection

(1) What are ways that the evil one takes Jesus' statements and uses them to shame you and confuse you about the Father's heart?

(2) What is the difference between "family embarrassment" and "condemnation?"

(3) What is your deepest fear? How would it change if you knew the Father's acceptance as Jesus does?

(4) What is the difference between your "identity" and your "experience?"

(5) In what ways has your service for others actually been for your own benefit?

(6) Can you hear Jesus saying to you, "Bring your religion to the fire of the Father's embrace. Put the ledger down. Throw your paintbrushes away and learn from me, for I know the Father, and I am gentle and humble in heart?"

(7) Why does Jesus tell us that he is gentle and humble in heart?

(8) Why do we resist Jesus?

(9) What do you think happens to you when you die?

The Back Porch Revisited

Jan was having an afternoon coffee when it happened. She was watching a cardinal as she stood at the kitchen sink, looking out into the cold, steely sky. The blast rocked the house. She felt the concussion on her face as the hair on her neck bristled. The kitchen windows rattled to the brink of shattering. She dropped her coffee cup as the fear of years shot through her heart. It could only have been one thing. She ran for the stairs. In a flash, Jan topped the stairs and turned for John's office. The door was closed, as if the whole world had been shut out. Jan's hand was shaking so terribly she could hardly turn the knob, but she did.

Then she saw it. First, John's arm on the floor, then blood. His favorite camel's hair coat looked like a sponge. Blood, blood, blood everywhere. Jan screamed: "Oh God! No! Please God, not this. Oh God, help me. Please God, no!"

She fell to her knees beside John, screaming as she lifted his head into her lap, rocking back and forth, as if it might help—crying, praying, cursing. *"Dammit,* John, what have you done, what have you done? Oh God, no! Not now. We have come so far."

She rocked, crying, frozen in the horror of it all. Then she saw the note, precisely folded on the floor by John's tan leather chair.

John had been depressed for months—years, really. He had fought nobly, but the knot in his gut had its own life. At times it was as big as Western Australia. He could never beat it. It was like a stray cat—always hanging around. And if you ever looked at the damned thing, it was moving in for good.

John had met Jan five years ago at a crawfish boil. His head was thrown back as he roared with laughter at some joke. When the laughter slowed, John looked down at the crawfish pot and then glanced inside the house. There Jan stood, shining in a light blue summer dress—blond hair, green eyes, a stunner. They met and ended up sitting on the swing for an hour or so, talking. Not a day had passed since then that they hadn't been together. Yet even with Jan, John still felt horribly alone, as he had throughout his first marriage. He loved Jan, but her love could scarcely get inside his heart. He tried, God knows he tried—therapy, AA, more therapy, even church—but the deep healing he so desperately wanted remained a mere hint in the wind. The terrible knot in his gut, relentless as the sea, never abated.

Jan,

You found me in the dark. You saved me for a while. We danced. But I can't do it anymore. I'm sorry, but I have to end this pain.

I love you,
John

John folded the note, picked up his 1911 model Colt 45, cocked it, and everything in the universe slowed down. He could feel the hard, cold trigger against his finger. He saw sweat drop from his brow. He heard the click, then the blast. He saw himself falling to the floor.

There was silence.

Flat on his back, John opened his eyes and looked up. He saw trees. *"Trees?* It didn't work, *dammit,* it didn't work!"

"Where am I? How did I get here? Am I at deer camp?"

It was minutes before dawn, light enough to see trees, but not light enough to understand. John could smell the earth, the leaves, the damp of the deep woods. He had no idea what was going on, or where he was, but he was still alive, his head was still there, and the old pain hadn't bothered to stay behind in his office.

"I hear a bark," John thought. "It is way off in the distance. There it is again, and again. It sounds so familiar, but how could it?"

It was definitely a dog, and it was headed John's way. "Maybe I *am* at deer camp," he thought, "but we never use dogs." Another bark, deep and rich and familiar.

Tears rolled down John's cheeks as an ancient joy rose within his soul.

"It couldn't be, but I know it is. *Charlie!*"

Within seconds, a black and white flash rounded a huge oak. Ears pinned back in the wind, Charlie ran like a racehorse straight for John. John tried to get up, but Charlie dove into his lap—barking, licking his face wildly. Clueless but thrilled, John hugged Charlie, grabbed his face and stared hard into his dancing eyes.

"This *is* Charlie. How could this be? *Where* am I?"

For a moment, all the pain was gone, the sadness, the terrible knot. The endless whisper was silenced as Charlie licked John's face, his tail wagging like a propeller.

"What is going on?" John asked himself.

He sat up, crying and laughing and silent all at the same time. Hugging Charlie, he looked into the woods. Dawn was here. It wasn't cold and it wasn't hot, and John had no idea where he was, but this place was more real than anything he had ever known.

"I must be dreaming. This can't be happening."

But it was.

"Charlie is real enough," John pondered, as he grabbed some leaves and dirt with his left hand. Staring at his hand, he smelled the leaves. His mind drifted back through the years, as he remembered his grandfather burning leaves in his backyard. That smell had always been John's favorite. Something about it gave him hope. That same hope, so lost through the years, was back. John smelled it in the leaves and in the dirt. He could hear it singing in the trees. He saw it in Charlie's eyes.

Charlie jumped up, ran about 20 yards, and stopped. Barking intensely, he motioned with his head for John to follow. John gathered himself, brushed off, wiped the dirt off on his pants, and started toward Charlie. Looking down, as if checking himself, he wondered, "Where is my camel's hair coat?"

Then he noticed something strange, really strange: His wedding ring was black. Not dark; it was black—jet black, shade 51 black. He rubbed it, but the black was not from dirt. The ring had changed color.

Charlie barked again and ran another 20 or so yards. John followed, moved by something deeper than the push of fear. He was thirsty and lost, lost as a man with a broken compass, but he had Charlie. How Charlie was here, how *he* was here, wherever *here* was, he hadn't a clue, but Charlie obviously knew his way around. Between steps, a twinge of the old pain stole into John's soul.

Within minutes, Charlie had John standing by a creek. Charlie stood silent beside a huge, flat rock, clearly leading John to sit and have a drink. "I knew Charlie was smart," John thought, "but this is eerie. It's as if he can read my mind."

John knelt and drank his fill. The water was clear and cool and soft as a spring breeze. For some reason, it reminded him of Jan's hair. Pain shot through his heart as he realized what he had done to her. "Where is she?" he wondered. "By now she is plain-out angry at me. God I am sorry," he cried out loud.

"But not really," a voice behind him spoke.

The voice scared the willies out of John. He had never heard a voice like that. "Who said that?" John asked himself, half hoping it was not real. He wanted to turn around, but he couldn't. Whoever spoke was real—very, very real. His voice was simple and deep, and those three words somehow spoke volumes.

"John," the voice called out, "we need to talk."

John froze in fear. Whoever it was behind him was no lightweight. "I am in the deep stuff!" He glanced at Charlie for comfort. Charlie had the most amazing look on his face. It was quizzical. No, it was more of a proud look. "I swear," thought John, "Charlie is smarter than ever. He looks like the cat that ate the canary. He is so proud of himself, he could burst. He knows something I don't."

At length, John looked around to face the voice. He saw feet first. "It is definitely a man," he mumbled to himself, "but *sandals?* Who wears sandals in the woods?"

"These are my woods," the voice said simply.

The voice was so true, so real, so assuring, it was scary.

John completed his turn, but kept his eyes down. A moment passed, then he felt a firm hand on his shoulder. "Rise, *My beloved*, receive My love and live."

Something like electricity shot through John's veins. He dared not look up, yet what fool would disobey this voice and this command? *"Who is this?"* John asked himself. "How does he know me? Surely he can't mean *me? I* am not lovable."

"John," the voice said, "My love defines what is lovable."

Unknown hope swept into John's heart. Slowly, but decidedly, John rose to his feet. Standing tall, but afraid, he at last opened his eyes. Before him stood a man, a simple man, but strong as an ox. His eyes were clear and ancient, full of compassion, yet unyielding.

"John," said the man, "you do not know who you are."

With that, Charlie barked. If he'd had hands, he would have been clapping, as if to say, *"Wake up."*

"Think back to the day Charlie died."

"I will never forget that day," John said, glancing down at Charlie.

"Remember the pain," said the man.

"I've never lived a day without that pain. I don't need to remember it."

"Close your eyes and watch the whisper steal its way into your soul."

"How do you see a whisper? Where do I look?"

"Stand on the back porch, close your eyes, and just watch."

"I can see myself crying," John said, "but I don't see anyone whispering."

"Keep looking."

"I don't see anything."

"Be still and watch."

"I can see it, I can see it!" John shouted.

"Now, think of the note you left for Jan before you shot yourself. What do you see in your heart?"

"I see nothing."

"What color is the nothingness, John?"

"I see black," John said.

"Look close. Pay attention."

"I still see only black."

"Keep looking."

"The black is moving. It is saying something."

"What is it saying, John?"

"I don't know, but it is definitely whispering something. It hurts like hell to listen. I can't bear this. Why didn't I die? Why am I still alive?"

"Take a deep breath and use my courage, John. *Rest!*"

John sat down. The burden of a thousand years was loosening.

"Why did you sit down, John?"

"Because you told me to rest."

"Do you now see what happens when you listen to my voice?"

The man knelt down and sat beside John. Looking deep into John's eyes, he asked, "What is the blackness whispering?"

"All I can hear is, 'I am not.'"

"Not *what*, John?"

"Not valuable, not important, not good enough, not special. It seems endless, but the same. I am not acceptable."

"John, is the whisper my voice?"

"No!"

"Whose is it?"

"I don't know."

"Why do you listen to it?"

"Well, it's true, isn't it?"

"Only true in your own mind, John—and nowhere else. My love defines what is true." Charlie barked again, grinning from ear to ear, almost laughing.

"When you look at the whisper, what do you feel, John?"

"Trapped!" John shouted. "I feel trapped, like I am on a ride at the fair that I hate and cannot get off. There is no 'stop' button, no exit ramp, no escape."

"Now go back to your note. What do you see in your heart?"

"It's the black whisper. It's all over the place, like a cancer in my heart."

"You *married* it, John."

"Married it! What do you mean? How can you marry a whisper?"

"You took it to be your bride. You opened your soul to it. You vowed to love it. And you did, John, you loved it."

"How? How did I love the whisper?"

"You believed the whisper as truth. You heard its echo everywhere. You saw its lie reflected on people's faces. You gave yourself to it."

"So that's why my wedding ring is black?"

"Yes, John. It is a symbol of your secret marriage—a marriage that must now be broken. John, do you see now why you won't let My Father love you?"

"Wait a minute," John shouted politely, "wait, wait, wait. What do you mean, *My Father?* That would mean you are the Son—that you are *Jesus?"*

"Who do you think I am, John?"

"I don't know, but you can't be Jesus. At least, you are nothing like the Jesus I always heard about."

"John, look at me. I am Jesus Christ, the Father's Son. Never mind now what you were told about me. Look into my eyes. What do you see, John?"

"Not black! I see sheer goodness. I see beauty—life."

"Have you seen this goodness before? Have you seen this beauty, this life?"

"Well, yes, I have, I've seen it a thousand times, but I never thought any of it was from you. I thought you were all about rules."

"My goodness, my beauty, my life are everywhere. I want you to participate in my life with me, John. I have always shared myself with you, but you were so confused and hurt, you could not see it. Think of Jan. You know you love her. Where does your love come from? Did you create love?"

"I have never thought about that. How could I create love?"

"John, listen. There is only one love in the universe, the love of the Father, Son, and Spirit. This love is shared with everyone. I see to that personally. The Father's dream is for you and the whole world to be filled to overflowing with our love, with our life, with our goodness and beauty. He wants you to receive His love for you, learn to live in its joy, and then to love others with His love. This is why I became human, John."

"But what about this pain? Where does this knot come from?"

"You already have the answer, John."

"The *whisper?*"

"Yes and no. What you call the 'knot in your gut' is three different pains coming together. The first pain is from me. It is the pain of the Father's love."

"I don't understand. How could the Father's love cause pain? It would seem to me to be the most wonderful thing in the universe."

"It is, John. The Father's love is the river of life running through all things. But it does cause pain for those in the dark."

"How does that work?"

"Think about forgiveness, John. When Jan says to you, 'I forgive you,' you know that means you have done something wrong, don't you? Forgiveness reveals guilt. The Father's forgiveness exposes your guilt. It is the same with the Father's beauty. His beauty exposes the ugliness you have made of your life."

"But what about the Father's love? How does His love cause pain?"

"John, as I share my own knowledge of the Father's love with you, you feel both hope and sadness. Tasting the Father's love shows you who you really are, and you feel its joy, but it also shows you how far you are from living in it. In that moment, you feel sadness. Just as my Father's forgiveness reveals your guilt, and His beauty reveals the mess, His love reveals you are sad."

"Forgive me, but that seems a bit unfair. Why share the Father's love with us at all, if it is only going to make us sad?"

"The point is never sadness, John. The Father only knows how to love. He's always about life, always determined that you know His love completely."

"So the pain comes from the places in my heart where I will not receive the Father's love?"

"Exactly, just as your joy comes from the places where you are receiving His love. I am faithful to show you where and when and how you are not receiving His lavish embrace. As I do, it causes pain in you."

"It is easy to see now how people have misunderstood you; you give them hope and make them sad at the same time. Well, it is not exactly *you* that makes them sad; it's the light of your love, is that right?"

"Yes, John, that is right. As I share my own knowledge of the Father's love, it exposes where people are bound up in the darkness. The exposure is the source of the pain."

"So if we weren't caught in the whisper, there would be no pain?"

"How could there be, John? The Father only knows how to love."

"So if everyone let the Father love them, there would be no sorrow?"

"I know the Father's love, John. Do you see any sorrow in me?"

"I think I am beginning to understand. The Father loves us, but we do not get it, or we do and we don't at the same time. Living life without receiving the Father's love means we are living life in . . . what is the opposite of receiving the Father's love?"

"Fear."

"So I have tried to live my life from fear rather than from the Father's love?

"Yes. Now what are the sisters of fear?"

"Anxiety, for sure. And then I would say hopelessness, insecurity, dread—*the knot in my gut!*"

"Yes!"

"But where does the fear come from?"

"Think, John, think. Does *fear* come from the Father's love? Does it have its origin in my heart, in the Spirit?"

"Of course not! But do I just create fear in my own mind?"

"Yes and no. It is a figment of your imagination all right, and it is very real to you, but fear does not originate with you at all.

"It comes from the black whisper, the 'I am not?'"

"Yes, John, fear starts with the whisper, but you give it a place in your life when you believe the whisper to be the truth. The whisper, the 'I am not,' is a lie. It has no basis in reality at all, until you receive it as real. Then you give it a place in your life, your world, your relationships."

"So if I could learn to ignore the whisper, fear would go away, and I could receive the Father's love?"

"Yes and no. It's time now for some proper theology."

"Theology!?"

"Yes, John, yours is terrible. The whisper does more than tell you 'I am not' and jump-start fear in your heart. The whisper, your faith in it, and the fear work together to redefine your idea of God."

"How do you mean?"

"You mentioned rules earlier, John."

"Yeah."

"Who told you I was about rules?"

"The preacher, the Sunday School teacher, everybody I know thinks that about you."

"But why would anyone believe that about my Father and me?"

"It just seems so obvious."

"But why, John, why does it seem so obvious to you that God is about rules?"

"Well, for one thing—I mean no disrespect, Sir—there are the 'Big Ten,' hanging in stone everywhere you look."

"Rules, John, always follow love. The Father loves; therefore he gives guidance as to how to receive His love and live in its joy. But why do people not see that the 'Big Ten,' as you called them, come on the heels of the best news in the universe, 'I am the Lord your God?' That is the Father speaking, John, declaring to Israel that He loves. So why do people skip right over His love and focus on the rules?"

"I have never thought about that before. Rules do follow love. Missing the Father's love, we are left with rules, rules we don't keep, so we are left with ourselves as failures. Good grief! I see it now. The whisperer takes our failure, uses it to redefine God in our heads, creates fear, and then whispers 'I am not' to us, which creates more fear. We have nowhere to go except, 'I am a failure, God couldn't possibly love me'—*the knot in my gut.*"

"You've got it, John."

"My whole life has been nothing but running from that knot. I tried to prove myself. I tried to drink the pain away. I tried to hide. I shut down and withdrew into my own world. I busied myself managing other people's inner world—what a mess—and it was all based on a lie, and the mess gives me more reason to fear."

"An endless circle."

"I think I am beginning to see the three pains. There is pain that comes from the Father's necessarily exposing love. There is pain from the 'I am not' whispered by the evil one. And there is pain from the mess we make of our lives and relationships, as we run and hide from the false god we have created under the influence of the whisper and its fear."

"Well done, John, well done."

"So, to stop the pain, we don't run from it—we face it, we feel it, we trace it back through our believing to its source, and we rethink our idea of God. Then we bring what we have done in the pain to the Father and receive His love again?"

"That is right, John, and you do what you can to make amends for the hurt you have caused in your pain."

"But what happens if we cannot see the Father? What happens if we get so caught in the darkness and its god that we cannot break through?"

"I will take care of that, John. I know the Father. I see His face, and by my own experience I know how to find you in the greatest darkness. I will always bring my knowledge of the Father into your heart. You must choose to embrace me, exposing love and all."

"How do you find me in my darkness?"

"That is a long story, John. For now just know the Holy Spirit is very smart, and in him, I am everywhere—everywhere. And remember, there would be no pain if I were not already inside your darkness."

"It's time now for you to go back, John."

"*Back!* But Jesus, if it's all the same to you, I would love to stay here for a while and talk with you. I have millions of questions. I have always wondered about heaven and hell."

"That is rather strange, isn't it, John, given where you've been and where you are? I know you have questions, and I have answers, and we have time. I will see to that."

"But you are so real to me here."

"Do you think I am not real there? I just told you, I am everywhere. I share my life with my Father in the fellowship of the Spirit with everyone. That's where your fellowship originates, your joy, your interests and burdens, your love. They all come from my knowledge of the Father's heart, which I share with the world.

"I will never leave you, John. I will never forsake you. I will always share myself and all I have with my Father with you. Don't run from me, especially when the Father's love hurts. Embrace me, give yourself to participate in my life.

"You will see me first in Jan's beautiful green eyes. After that, just listen and watch and live.

"Immanuel is not a theory, John. Don't let the whisperer lead you into death this time.

"Read your namesake, John, read your namesake—14:20."

Charlie jumped into John's lap and licked his face. His eyes glowed with shameless delight, the happiest dog in the universe. John gave Charlie a long hug, whispering something in his ear as he said goodbye. John turned again toward Jesus. Putting his right hand on John's shoulder, Jesus spoke: "Rise, *My beloved,* receive My love and live."

John felt Jan shaking him. *"John! John!* You're snoring so loud it could wake the dead. *Wake up! Wake up!"*

Opening his eyes, John couldn't believe it when he saw Jan's face. He did a double take and stared hard into her green eyes, smiling to himself.

"You must have been dreaming something good. I mean, between the snores and all."

"Yeah, Jan, you won't believe it. I had the most amazing dream: I met Jesus himself, and I saw my old dog Charlie." John shook his head, half laughing, half trying to understand. He wasn't sure it was a dream. He checked the back of his head, glanced at his camel's hair coat and looked again at Jan.

"What? Why are you looking at me that way?"

"Sorry, Jan, I don't mean anything by it. I guess I was just making sure this is real."

"Real? Why would it not be real, John?"

"Do you know John 14:20?"

"No, why?"

"We'll have a long, long talk tomorrow. Right now I am exhausted."

John caught a flash of his ring as he reached for Jan's hand—gold, solid gold, shining like the sun. He grinned, shook his head and laughed again, thinking of that look on Charlie's face.

John put his arms around Jan, kissed her on the cheek, and squeezed her. Staring again into her green eyes, he whispered, "God, I love your eyes."

"For the first time in years, I want to live, I *want* to live, and now I *know how.* I will tell you all about it."

They walked to the bedroom. As he reached to turn off the lights, John heard barking deep in the woods.

"John?" Jan asked, interrupting his thoughts, "Did you work in the yard today?"

"No. Why do you ask?"

"Just wondering—you have dirt under you fingernails."

Questions for Reflection

(1) Describe what you felt when Charlie rounded the tree and dove into John's lap. What do these feelings tell you about yourself? If you could talk to John, what would you ask him?

(2) What whisper have you married?

(3) What is the origin of your love? What about the love of the non-Christian mother for her children?

(4) Reflect carefully on the different parts of this statement: "John, listen. There is only one love in the universe, the love of the Father, Son, and Spirit. This love is shared with everyone. I see to that personally. The Father's dream is for you and the whole world to be filled to overflowing with our love, with our life, with our goodness and beauty. He wants you to receive His love for you, learn to live in its joy, and then to love others with His love. This is why I became human, John."

(5) What is the point of human history?

(6) In what ways will John's relationship with Jan change?

(7) How do you think the new John will fare with the church?

(8) Is spiritual pain an enemy to be avoided or a strange friend to be embraced? Why are we so afraid of facing our pain? Is religion an attempt to avoid our pain in the name of God?

(9) Do you think the Father, Son, and Spirit relate to you in your darkness, or to the version of you that you present to others?

(10) What is the greatest barrier to your letting the Father love you?

Suggestions for Further Reading

Athanasius. *On the Incarnation.* London: A. R. Mowbray & Comp., 1963.

Barth, Karl. "The Covenant as the Presupposition of Reconciliation." In *Church Dogmatics* IV/1. Edinburgh: T & T Clark, 1963, pp. 22–54.

_____. "The Way of the Son of God into the Far Country." In *Church Dogmatics* IV/1. Edinburgh: T & T Clark, 1963, pp. 157–211.

_____. "The Homecoming of the Son of Man." In *Church Dogmatics* IV/2, Edinburgh: T & T Clark, 1963, pp. 36–116.

Blue, Ken. *Healing Spiritual Abuse.* Downers Grove: InterVarsity Press, 1993.

Capon, Robert Farrar. *Parables of Grace.* Grand Rapids: Eerdmans, 1988.

Eldredge, John. *Waking the Dead.* Nashville: Thomas Nelson Publishers, 2003.

Erskine, Thomas. *The Unconditional Freeness of the Gospel.* Edinburgh: Waugh and Innes, 1829. Also available at <www.perichoresis.org>.

Lewis, C. S. "The Weight of Glory." In *The Weight of Glory and Other Essays.* Grand Rapids: Eerdmans, 1965, pp. 1–15.

_____. *The Great Divorce.* New York: Collier Books, 1946.

_____. *Till We Have Faces.* New York: Harcourt Brace Jovanovich, 1980.

MacDonald, George. *The Complete Fairy Tales.* London: Penguin Books, 1999.

Manning, Brennan. *Abba's Child.* Colorado Springs: NavPress, 2002.

Payne, Leanne. *The Healing Presence.* Grand Rapids: Baker Books, 1989.

Smail, Thomas. *The Forgotten Father.* London: Hodder and Stoughton, 1987.

_____. *Once and For All: A Confession of the Cross.* Eugene: Wipf & Stock, 1998 Torrance, J. B. *Worship, Community and the Triune God of Grace.* Downers Grove: IVP, 1996.

Torrance, J. B. *Worship, Community and the Triune God of Grace.* Downers Grove: InterVarsity Press, 1996.

Torrance , T. F. *The Mediation of Christ.* Grand Rapids: Eerdmans, 1983.

_____. *Preaching Christ Today*. Grand Rapids: Eerdmans, 1994.

_____. "The Resurrection and the Person of Christ" and "The Resurrection and
  the Atoning Work of Christ." In *Space, Time and Resurrection*.
  Edinburgh: The Handsel Press, 1976, pp. 46–84.

_____. *The Trinitarian Faith: The Evangelical Theology of the Ancient Catholic
  Church*. Edinburgh: T & T Clark, 1988.

For an extended reading list, please visit our website: <www.perichoresis.org>.

CPSIA information can be obtained at www.ICGtesting.com
Printed in the USA
LVOW120228171211

259765LV00002B/329/P